HELP YOURSELF

An everyday survival handbook

Alastair Thomson and
Rosemary Platt

impact books

First published in Great Britain 1985
by **impact books**,
112 Bolingbroke Grove, London SW11 1DA

Phototypeset by Sunrise Setting, Torquay, Devon.
Printed and bound in Great Britain by
Whitstable Litho Ltd., Whitstable, Kent.

British Library Cataloguing in Publication Data

Thomson, Alastair
Help yourself: an everyday survival handbook.
1. Living alone — Great Britain
2. Social adjustment
I. Title
II. Platt, Rosemary
306.8'8   HQ800.4.G7

ISBN 0–245–54281–7

Contents

Acknowledgements

We'd like to say thanks to Grant Goddard who was there when the idea for this book first came up, to Ros Morpeth and Tom Goodison who, in different ways, gave us the opportunity to look into some of the issues more deeply and to Jean-Luc Barbanneau for his support and work in making *Help Yourself* a reality.

Many organisations and individuals have helped with information – our thanks to them and apologies for any misinterpretations. Finally we recognise our debt to all the individuals with whom we've worked whose questions and curiosity led us to write it.

Introduction

This book is an information guide – some of the things in it we've needed to find out both for ourselves or for people we've known. We hope it helps you to help yourself too by covering a broad range of topics with follow-up suggestions. No book as wide ranging as *Help Yourself* can be perfect: some things you want to know may not be covered, you may not like some of the things we've said and you may spot a mistake (although we've made every effort to check all our facts).

We don't pretend to know it all and would be glad to hear of any suggestions of how the book could be improved. But in the meantime, always check the information since things do change. If you write to any of the organizations mentioned, think about enclosing a s.a.e. – some of them operate on low budgets.

Most of the material in *Help Yourself* applies to everyone but we've tried to include things of particular relevance to young people and are pleased that the book is published in 1985 – International Youth Year, to which it is our contribution.

Good luck.

Alastair Thomson
Rosemary Platt

1. Getting a job

The problem ■ looking for work ■ what job do you want? ■ your curriculum vitae ■ applying for jobs ■ going for interviews ■ help and advice

The problem

Although there are quite a few books around which aim to help you find a job, most of them seem to assume that if you do what they suggest, then you'll get one. This is a con – it makes you feel that you must have done something wrong or there's something the matter with you if you fail to get work. Although there *are* skills which you need to learn, it's important to be clear, right from the start:

> **There are tens of thousands more people looking for work than there are jobs available.**

This means that if you're looking for employment or if you're having no luck in changing your job, it's unlikely to be your fault if you're not successful.

Unemployment is higher than at any time in the past fifty years. What's becoming clear is that we will probably never return to a time when everyone who wants to work can get a permanent, full-time, paid job from when they leave education to when they retire. This means that many of our ideas about work are going to have to change. Chapter 3 (*Beating unemployment*) looks at what's happening to work and the ways you can live through the changes, but in the meantime there are many ways you can improve your chances if you're looking for work.

When lots of people are looking for work, employers get more choosy about who to take on. This means you have to try harder. The advice in this chapter isn't a magic formula but it does outline the things you must think about if you're to help yourself find paid work. Some of the things seem really obvious – but it's surprising just how much you can forget if you're filling in forms in a hurry or

if you're very nervous about an interview. Even if you're fairly
confident, you can still use the information as a checklist to make
sure you're prepared.

Looking for work

This is boring, repetitive and can get downright depressing. But
don't give up. When it comes down to it, getting a job today is often
simply a matter of being in the right place at the right time – and
that's why it's important to keep on trying: if employers don't even
know you exist, they can hardly offer you work.

Profile
"I filled in about fifty application forms before I even got an
interview. I'd just about given up hope and thought I'd be stuck
where I was forever. But then I had three interviews in two weeks. I
got very depressed when I didn't get the job at any of them but I
went on trying and finally got what I wanted. It took about eight
months in all – and I had the right sort of experience and
qualifications."

(Linda, 24, teacher)

Probably your best bets when you look for work are to:
- make sure you're looking in all the places that advertise the kind
  of job you want.
- look regularly if you're serious.
- get the first editions (lunchtime ones) of local papers if they have
  your sort of jobs – don't leave it until the evening.
- make sure you have the right sort of qualifications for the jobs –
  be realistic about what you are likely to get (even if you know
  you deserve better).

The sorts of places you'll need to look depend very much on the sort
of work you are able and willing to do.

The Careers Service
This is primarily for people under nineteen. It is run by the local
education authority in every area and its job is to:
- try and match people up with the jobs that local employers tell
  them are available.

■ offer advice and information about the skills, interests and qualifications you need for particular jobs.
■ tell people about education and training and about local employers.

You'll be disappointed though if you expect Careers Officers to tell you what sort of job you should do – only you can decide that. What they can offer is accurate and impartial information and personal attention.

Once you're over nineteen, you'll be lucky to get very much help unless you've just left education. In some areas the Careers Service refuses point blank to help adults, in others they'll see you if they have time. Probably the most you can expect is to be allowed to use their information services.

To find your nearest Careers Office, look in the phone book under "CAREERS". Some are happy for people to drop in, others like you to make an appointment.

Jobcentres and Employment Offices

These are mainly for people over nineteen but most are helpful to younger people as well. There are about a thousand centres throughout the country which have details of jobs in their areas. What they do is display details of vacancies on display boards, grouped according to the type of work. You can go in and browse around to see what's available. If something looks interesting you note its reference number and ask one of the staff behind the desks to tell you more about it. They will often ring up employers for you and fix up interviews if the job is still available. People under nineteen who are unemployed have to register at the Jobcentre, Employment Office or with the Careers Service in order to claim supplementary benefit. Other people can register if they want – but unless you've got an unusual skill there's often not much point.

As well as displaying vacancies, Jobcentres have details of schemes for unemployed people and training opportunities (including special help for disabled people).

Although the "self-service" approach of Jobcentres means it's easy to drop in and look round, the drawback is that they can't really give you any personal attention or advice about employment. The big problem however, is that in many areas, the number of jobs they are able to display is depressingly low – often the boards are almost empty. This means there's not much incentive to go in regularly and it's easy to stop bothering.

Jobcentres and Employment Offices are listed in the phone book under "MANPOWER SERVICES COMMISSION" (the organisation which runs them).

Professional and Executive Recruitment

If you've been working in a professional, executive or scientific job you can register with Professional and Executive Recruitment (PER) at your Jobcentre or Employment Office. You can also register if you've got A-levels, Scottish Highers, a degree or equivalent qualifications. PER is run by the Manpower Services Commission – the same organisation which runs Jobcentres. When you enrol, you'll be sent a copy of their *Job Hunting Handbook* and, unless you're straight from education, weekly copies of their newspaper *Executive Post* – which contains hundreds of different jobs at managerial level. New graduates get sent *Graduate Post* – a fortnightly newspaper of vacancies.

Everyone who enrols with PER is invited to a free half-day job-hunting seminar – which provides information on the job market and tips on how to sell yourself to employers.

Ask at the Jobcentre or Employment Office if you think you should be eligible – you can register even if you've got a job.

Employment Agencies

These are private companies which charge employers for filling their vacancies. You don't pay anything. To use their services you have to register with them. They take details of your experience and qualifications and try to match you up to a vacancy. Most agencies deal with particular types of work (such as nursing or office work) and some specialise in temporary jobs – but you may find some that carry general vacancies. Obviously you'll be more in demand if you've got special skills.

You can find details of places in the yellow pages under "EMPLOYMENT AGENCIES".

Newspaper and magazine adverts

Local newspapers carry job adverts under a number of headings; "situations vacant", "general vacancies" and so on as well as under specific headings like "office work", "scientific and technical" or "catering". It's also worth looking under part–time vacancies too. If the paper comes out every day, you'll soon find which days have most adverts (Saturdays are dead, Mondays seem to be pretty slack but Thursdays always seem popular) – but the most important thing is to get the paper early and phone or write for details as soon as you can. Be prepared – there are still jobs where the employers may ask you along straight away or may interview you over the phone. Local papers every day can cost you more than you can afford – but waiting until the library gets its copy may be too late.

You can use the library to check jobs in the national papers. If you don't mind where you work, these can be a good bet although the majority are for skilled posts. Some papers have different sorts of jobs each day so you'll soon work out the most useful times to look. Competition for jobs advertised nationally is likely to be pretty stiff – so you may need all the self–confidence you've got if you want to follow them through.

Some magazines you can buy in shops carry job ads. *The Lady* for example has quite a few child care jobs, *Melody Maker* for musicians – but often with no pay guaranteed! Londoners will also find quite a few jobs in *Time Out* and *City Limits*. There are also other special magazines which newsagents don't usually display – these are trade magazines or papers. Produced for people working in particular jobs, these quite often have vacancy adverts – but the problem is finding them since libraries won't usually get them. Probably your best bet is to find someone working in the sort of occupation that interests you and and see if they'll lend you their copy (it's a good way to find out more about the occupation anyway). Examples of trade papers include *British Baker, The Bookseller, Community Care* and *Nursery World*.

Finally, remember you could try placing an advert under "situations wanted" yourself – you might just strike lucky. You could also try putting cards in local newsagent windows, this can sometimes lead to odd bits of part–time work in things like mowing lawns or babysitting while you're trying for something full–time.

Contacting employers

You don't have to wait around to hear about jobs – you can also contact local employers by writing to them or visiting. Most times you'll find they won't have any vacancies but you can ask that they bear you in mind in case something does come up.

Use the Careers Service and yellow pages to find the details of places that sound right to approach.

In you write:

■ do each letter individually (whether you write or type, never send a photocopied letter or the employer will simply think you're not really bothered)

■ keep your letter short – just say why you're writing, what you're looking for and that you're enclosing details about yourself

■ include a copy of your CV (see below) – this can be a photocopy

■ ask that they keep your details on file if there's nothing suitable just now.

If you visit:

■ dress neatly, you might get invited for a chat there and then

■ try to get past receptionists and secretaries to see the person who is actually responsible for recruitment (say you'll wait until the person's free if you have to)

■ take copies of your CV to leave with them if there's nothing suitable (they may prefer to contact you in future rather than advertise for someone).

Don't get depressed if this method of job-hunting doesn't seem to be getting you anywhere. Quite often your letters won't even get an acknowledgement or you won't be allowed to see the right person – even if you do, he or she may be fairly rude and abrupt. All the same, it could be that you have made a good impression and that your details will be remembered when something *does* come up in the future.

Family and friends

Make sure you tell *everyone* you know that you're looking for a job and the sort of work you want. Many vacancies are heard about "through the grapevine", with someone putting in a good word for a person they know. Some small employers prefer this sort of recommendation rather than going to the time, trouble and expense of advertising.

What job do you want?

Choosing what sort of work you'd like is never easy. Lots of people end up doing something they don't enjoy simply because someone else suggested it. When there's high unemployment, there's even more pressure on us – from other people who tell us to take whatever we can get and be grateful for it. It may be that you *would* be prepared to do any job – but you can't apply for everything and you're more likely to get the jobs which interest you, if only because you'll try harder and sound more enthusiastic. This means you have to make some choices.

Whatever your decisions, you'll probably feel happier about them if you've worked out the choices for yourself. But in order to choose, you need to be properly informed:

■ about yourself
■ about what particular jobs involve and the skills and qualifications you may need
■ about the chances of finding work in those jobs – both locally and nationally.

Look at yourself

This may sound a bit funny – after all, you probably know yourself better than anyone else! But have you really thought out what you want from life and what you would expect a job to give you? Lots of people will start off by answering "MONEY" – but there's usually more to it than this.

Try answering the following questions and writing what you want on a bit of paper. This may jog you into thinking up more things for yourself.

Do you want:

■ the worries and demands of high pressure jobs or a quiet life?
■ reasonable security or the chance to take risks?
■ a job which interests you or one that gives you time to follow your interests outside work?
■ a job which you think is useful to other people or one that just pays well?
■ a job with low pay but a high status or one that's got less prestige but better pay?
■ a low paid, boring job with promotion prospects or a more interesting job with higher pay but no future?
■ jobs offering companionship and teamwork or ones where you're on your own?
■ jobs with predictable hours or ones where the hours can change with not much warning?

When you look at what you've written, you may be surprised – think about it carefully though and try to see why. Also, see if you can clarify any questions you've answered with "it depends" – what *are* the things on which it depends?

The next step is to try and list in order of priority which things are most important. When you've done this, try to make similar lists for:
– the sort of things you're good at;
– the sort of things you enjoy (these lists are often different!).
What all this can give you is a better understanding of your motivation and skills – in a way that will help you compare various sorts of work to see how well or badly they meet your expectations and abilities.

Find out about jobs

There are probably all sorts of jobs about which you know nothing – you may even not have heard of them. Only by talking to people about their jobs, by using the careers books in your library and asking at the Careers Service can you expect to decide which sorts of work best suits what you want and what you have to offer. Remember too, while you're doing your research, that very few people can honestly say that they like everything about their work all the time. Most jobs have bits people don't enjoy – the question is whether the plus points outweigh the minus ones!

Measure your chances

Talk to Careers Officers about your chances of getting the sorts of job which interest you. They may be able to suggest training courses or experience that will improve your prospects – or tell you the right sort of places to look (after all, different jobs are to be found in different areas and have their own patterns of recruitment). If your chances aren't very good you'll have to decide whether to try for something else or work to improve them – some jobs are easier to find as you get older for instance.

Whatever sort of work you choose, remember that you've not committed yourself for ever. More and more people are changing careers during their lives. You may even decide that a full-time job working for someone else isn't what you want at all – in which case look at Chapter 3.

Your curriculum vitae (CV)

Sometimes called a "personal information chart", this is one of your most important aids in job-hunting. It's one or two sheets of paper on which you've collected the key facts about your life and experience (curriculum vitae is Latin for "life course").

Sometimes adverts ask you to "reply with CV and letter of application". Sometimes you'll want to send it out when you write to employers on spec and you'll always find it useful to consult when you fill in forms. Unless it's absolutely impossible, you should type your CV or find someone who can do it for you – it'll look a lot smarter. Once you have written it, you'll find it worthwhile to have a few photocopies made so you don't need to start from scratch each time you need it.

Lots of applications are written under pressure and occasionally things get forgotten – that's why it's worth taking the time (even if you're not actually looking for work now) to perfect your CV in advance. You can always update and improve it as needed. Many people find CVs difficult to write, they can't think of much to say about themselves. If that's the case for you, ask for help from family or friends who know you well – it's often useful to see ourselves through the eyes of other people. In addition, it's always worth letting someone read through what you put to check for spelling mistakes.

Exactly what should go in your CV will vary according to where your career path has led you. If you're looking for your first job you'll want to include some things which you'll be able to drop (unless still relevant) when you're more experienced. Your CV should not expand indefinitely. Unless you've had an extraordinarily eventful life, it's best to keep it down to two sides of paper or less. For example, the paper round or Saturday job you mention when you're seventeen can probably be forgotten when you're twenty. Likewise, your membership of the school debating club isn't going to be of interest to employers once you've been out of school a year or so.

Your CV checklist
There are various ways in which you can organise your information but this way is very common:

A heading ("JEAN PETERS; PERSONAL INFORMATION" for example)

Personal details
- your name (either underline your family name or write it first since that's how your CV will be filed)
- your home address (include the postcode – it shows you're efficient!)
- your home phone number (and a work number if you have one)
- your age and date of birth
- your status (whether you're single, married or divorced)
- your dependents (the number of children you may have, plus their ages)
- your nationality
- your health (either say you're in good health or mention any disability you have)

Education and training
- the names and towns of the schools or colleges you went to after the age of eleven.
- details of all the qualifications you have, together with the grades and the year in which they were awarded. If you're still waiting for any results, say so. If you've not got any qualifications then you could put the subjects you were best at or enjoyed.
- remember to put any part-time courses you've attended – perhaps as part of your work, any training schemes you've been on and any evening classes that are more than just leisure activities.

Employment history
- this should cover all full-time jobs you've ever had (if you've done a lot of casual work, you may find it easier to group them together by writing something like "1980 – May 1982, unskilled builders' labourer, various employers". Otherwise say what each job was, who it was for and the dates when you did it.
- unless it's obvious from the job title what you did, it may help to give a one or two sentence explanation of your responsibilities.
- list all your part-time jobs and any work experience you've done if you're looking for your first or second full-time posts. Once you've worked for a while you may decide to just mention part-time holiday jobs briefly – or even drop them altogether.

- the CV shouldn't have any gaps, so if you've had periods of unemployment it's best to put them in too.
- include any long-term periods of voluntary work even if you weren't paid.

Other information
- some people just call this bit "Activities and interests". You should mention these (membership of clubs or sports teams, any voluntary work you do, hobbies and so on) but there are other things too.
- put down if you've got a driving licence, first aid certificate or anything else useful.
- you may also want to mention any equipment you can use (word processor, telephone switchboard, lathes and so on).

Referees
- put the names, addresses and job titles of two people (not family) who've agreed to write about you if asked by employers.
- if you're working, one of the two should be your current employer.
- if you've just left education one person should be your old head teacher or a college lecturer.

When it's finished, your CV should look something like the one on the next page.

Applying for jobs

Remember that first impressions may count for a lot – so take care whether you're writing a letter, visiting, filling in a form or making a phone call. With so many people chasing so few jobs, employers will be looking for any reason to reduce the number of applicants they consider. This means that things like neatness do matter.

Letters
There are essentially two sorts of job-hunting letter:
- the short letter asking for an application form or more details about a job.
- the letter of application (which may be accompanied by your CV – see above) in which you say why you want the job and why you think you are suitable.

<u>CURRICULUM VITAE: JAYNE LAWTON</u>

<u>Personal details</u>

Name: Jayne Christine <u>Lawton</u>

Address: 22 Green Lane, Millbank, Stanton, Beckhamshire
                         BC44 8QQ

Home telephone: Stanton (0101) 234567

Date of Birth: 7th February 1967   (Aged 18 years)

Marital status: Single

Nationality: British

Health: Good

<u>Education and training</u>

1978 - 1983: Stanton School for Girls

1983 to date: Stanton College of Further Education (2 year secretarial course).

<u>Qualifications</u>

GCE O-levels (1983):	English Language	grade B
	Physics	grade B
	English Literature	grade C
	Maths	grade D
CSE (1983):	Geography	grade 1
	French	grade 1
	Human Biology	grade 2
	History	grade 3
Royal Society of Arts Certificates (1984)	Typewriting	stage 2
	Shorthand	80 words per minute
	Secretarial duties	stage 1

This summer I shall be taking A-level Communications and hope to have
achieved RSA stage 3 in typing and shorthand up to 100 words per minute.

<u>Experience</u>

Between August 1981 and May 1982, I had a daily paper round with Mitchells
Newsagents of Stanton. In February 1983 I did one week of work experience
in the offices of Spurlings Ltd. of Kelston and since June 1983, I have
worked as an assistant at Webster and Bilton Ltd. on Saturdays and in my
vacations.

<u>Interests</u>

Since coming to college, I have developed an interest in drama and am now
Treasurer of the college drama group and have had parts in three plays.
I am also on the student union social committee. My other interests
include reading and badminton.

I am presently learning to drive a car and hope to take my test this year.

<u>Referees</u>

Mrs Lesley Herman, Head of Business Studies, Stanton College of Further
Education, Brick Lane, Stanton BC41 5KK.

Mr Wesley Hardy, General Manager, Webster and Bilton Ltd., Gold Street
Stanton BC44 6QW.

Of these, the first is by far the easiest, but there are a few rules you should remember for both types:

- Always make a rough copy of what you're going to say and if you can, ask someone to check it for spelling. Keep your copy because you might need to remember what you said if you get an interview.
- Stick to sheets of unlined white paper. Your Snoopy headed paper or a page from an exercise book isn't good enough.
- If you can type and set out a letter properly, then use your skill – if not, then write in blue or black ink or ballpoint, never in red or green. If you write and find keeping your lines straight a problem, put lined paper under your plain sheet.
- Put your address in the top right hand corner.
- Put the name and address of the employer in the top left hand corner. If you're writing to a particular person, put his or her job title after the name and before the address.
- Date the letter (beneath your address).
- If you start "Dear Sir or Madam" end with "Yours faithfully". If you start "Dear Mrs Brown" (or any other name) end with "Yours sincerely".
- Print your name under your signature (plus "Mr" or "Ms" in brackets if it's not clear whether you're a man or woman).
- Read through what you've written and if you can, get someone else to read it as well. If there are any mistakes, or if you think it could be better presented or worded, do it again!

Of the letters you may have to write, letters asking for forms or details are easy. They should be short and to the point, simply saying the post in which you're interested and where you heard about the job. Something like this will do:

> *Dear Sir/Madam,*
>
> *I would be grateful if you could send me details of the post of . . . . which was advertised in this week's "Evening Post", together with an application form.*
>
> *Yours faithfully, "*

Letters of application are more difficult. Sometimes they can be really frustrating, particularly when employers ask for "letters of application" or even specify that you should explain things like:

- what qualities you think you can bring to the job

- how you think the job fits into your career plan
- your strengths and weaknesses.

This is never easy. Try and get someone to help you – two minds are better than one on tasks like this. The guidelines below may help:

- Keep it short – no more than two sides is the absolute maximum (one is probably better) since anything too long may cause the person reading it to get bored. Remember you can always enclose your CV separately.
- Keep it to the point – read the advert or job description carefully and try to work out exactly what the employer is looking for.
- Start by saying why you're writing – something like: "I should like to apply for the post of . . . .".
- Make your main aim *to get an interview*. Don't put down everything you can think of – just try to get the employer interested. You may find it useful to end with a sentence like "I would be pleased to answer any questions at an interview" or "I look forward to the chance of an interview to answer any questions you may have".
- Ensure that you haven't written anything irrelevant or unnecessary.

Application forms

Any mistake on an application form sticks out like a sore thumb, so don't try to fill them in as soon as you get them. Read through them before you do anything and follow these suggestions:

- Check for instructions ("Write in black ink", "Block capitals", "Most recent experience first" for example).
- Either fill in the form in pencil first so you can correct mistakes or make a photocopy on which you can practise.
- For sections like "Previous experience" or "Reasons for application" plan out what you're going to say in rough and then copy it onto a sheet the same size as the space on the form so you can check it's not too long. Only after you've checked this should you write it out properly on the form.
- Don't leave sections blank – if you've nothing to say, write "none" or "not applicable" so that it doesn't look like you've missed something out.
- Check through what you've written for mistakes (it's easy to do something daft like writing this year, rather than the year you were born under "Date of Birth"!

■ Keep a copy of the form – or at least the bits you wrote under the "Reasons for application" section so that you can remind yourself of what you wrote if asked to an interview.

■ Try to give yourself plenty of time to fill in the form, you're less likely to scribble down mistakes this way.

Phone calls

A lot of people really hate having to use the phone when job-hunting. You're talking to someone you don't know and can't see – and there are no second chances. The only way you can overcome this hang-up is by good organisation. Have a clear idea of what you want to find out or what points you want to make – jot them down on paper if you need to. Make sure you've got the number, extension and job title of the person you want to contact, together with the details of the post you're interested in. If you have to ring from a call box, be sure to have enough change. Always have a pen and paper with you to write any points down – and remember to speak clearly and slowly – don't try to speak like you do when you ring friends!

If you have no luck

A few refusals are to be expected, but if you're making lots of applications and getting no response you'll have to look at your applications carefully. Of course it is possible that you're doing everything right and have just the right qualifications and experience and still don't get the job. This may be because the organisation already has someone in mind for the job and is simply advertising as a formality, it may also be because of discrimination (see the section *Help and advice* for how to challenge this). It may be the case though that you're going to have to look at your job-hunting strategy again:

■ Are you applying for jobs that are really beyond someone with your qualifications and experience? There's nothing wrong with aiming high but you must realise that doing so is a bit of a gamble. Try applying for other jobs that are at a lower level as well as the really ambitious ones.

■ Is there something wrong with your application technique? If you can't spot any faults, try asking other people to look through your applications or consult one of the specialist books listed at the end of the chapter.

Going for interviews

If you do get an interview, you're in with a fair chance since employers won't waste time seeing people who haven't a hope. Now you've got this far it's worth taking as much care as you can. As well as doing your best on the day you should use the time beforehand too.

Before the interview
- Write details of the time and place into your diary or on your calendar immediately – and remember them! Some people actually forget about interviews or turn up on the wrong day.
- Confirm that you will attend.
- Plan how you're going to get there – check maps or up to date bus and train timetables. Allow yourself plenty of time for the journey and aim to get to the place about fifteen minutes early. (If you're not sure how long it'll take or about the nearest bus stop, ask when you confirm your attendance.)
- Research exactly what the job involves and what the employer does. As well as studying any job description carefully, you could also use the library or Careers Service to find out more.
- Prepare the answers to the sort of questions you think they'll ask and think about what you want to ask about the job.

On the day
- Take the letter inviting you to attend so that you remember who to ask for when you get there.
- Dress smartly – even if it's the sort of job you would do in overalls or jeans.
- If for any reason you get delayed on the journey, ring the employer and explain what's happened.
- When you get there use the extra time you've allowed yourself to go to the loo if you need to, to look around and try and get the feel of the place and to read any leaflets or notices in the waiting room.
- Be polite to the reception or secretarial staff – it's not unknown for employers to ask their opinions.
- Don't smoke unless you have to.

In the interview

■ When you're asked in, put out your cigarette if you're smoking, try to smile and try to look confident – but don't grin like an idiot!

■ Wait until you're asked before sitting down (if they seem to have forgotten then ask). Don't perch on the edge of the chair but don't slouch back either.

■ Don't light up unless invited.

■ Try and take a few deep breaths if you're nervous.

■ Whether there's just one person asking questions or several, it'll usually start with introductions. Look at the person speaking and if you're afraid your voice will croak or squeak when the questions start, use the chance to say something like "pleased to meet you" or whatever – it does help.

Once you're settled and they've tried to relax you with a few questions about your journey or the weather, then the interview proper will begin. The sort of questions usually asked will cover:

■ your education and training

■ your past experience (don't look on this as a chance to slag off your past employer!)

■ your ambitions (sometimes they ask "where do you see yourself in five years time?")

■ why you have applied for the job (don't just answer "For the money" even if it's true!) and what you think it involves

■ the sort of skills you think you can bring to the job and how you'd approach it.

As well as listening to the answers, they'll be looking at your overall communication skills and trying to judge whether you'd fit in – so watch out that you don't start sounding bossy, arrogant and insensitive; in particular, don't waffle but do try to answer with more than a "yes" or a "no". If you're not sure what they mean by a question, say so – ask for them to repeat it, and don't be afraid to pause for thought.

The interviewer will also tell you a bit about the job and ask if you have any questions. If you've prepared properly, you should have two or three ideas (don't overdo it). Try to steer clear of questions about what you can get from the job – like money and holidays, though training opportunities is alright. Instead, use the chance to suggest what you could bring to the job or show your understanding of it.

It's unusual to be told immediately whether or not you've got the job – but if they don't say, you should ask when they'll let you know.

After the interview

If you've had to spend money on getting to the interview and nobody's mentioned anything, have a word with the secretary or receptionist about expenses. Once you've sorted that out, don't contact the employer again unless you've been asked to. If you don't hear anything, don't assume you've been forgotten – things may be going on behind the scenes and it may be a good sign for your chances.

When you finally hear the news you've got the job, contact the organisation to accept (or decline) the offer as soon as you can. If you hear that you've not got the job, then don't waste too much time grieving about it. Think through your performance to see if there were any things you could learn from (such as difficult questions) and then look to the future. Not many people succeed with their first interview and the chances are that in future you won't be so nervous. Don't give up hope.

Help and advice

Places

Most of the places you can get help are mentioned in the chapter but your most important sources of help and advice are:

■ the *Careers Service* (in the phonebook under "CAREERS").
■ the *local library* (good for newspapers and magazines with job adverts plus books about particular careers. If they haven't got what you want ask them to borrow it from another library).
■ the *National Advisory Centre on Careers for Women*, Drayton House, 30 Gordon Street, London WC1H 0AX. Tel: 01 380 0117. Advice service covering career changes, education choices and re-training. Appointment needed. Also ask about publications.

Disabled people can find specialist help and support plus details of special schemes to assist them in job-hunting from the Careers Service, Jobcentres and Employment Offices.

If you believe that you have experienced discrimination on the grounds of your race or sex when job-hunting, then the employer may have been breaking the law. Look at Chapter 7 of this book and seek advice from the Citizens' Advice Bureau, Law Centre or one of the other organisations listed in that chapter.

Publications

For help in deciding what sort of job you want, look at *What else can you do: a guide to job change and career planning* by Andrew Pates, Hilary Rosenberg and Alastair Thomson, published by the Careers and Occupational Information Centre, £2.50.

For details of specific jobs, look at *Equal Opportunities: a careers guide for Women and Men* by Ruth Miller and Anna Alston, published by Penguin Books, £4.95.

For a straightforward guide to job-hunting, look at *The Unemployment Handbook* by Guy Dauncey, published by the National Extension College, £2.25.

2. Working for a wage

Starting a job ■ contracts ■ money ■ trade unions ■ health and safety ■ dismissal – fair or unfair? ■ time off work ■ redundancy ■ pregnancy ■ problems at work ■ moving on ■ help and advice

Starting a job

You're likely to feel a bit nervous about starting a new job whether or not you've worked before. If you've simply moved to a new job you may have to change some of your ways but if it's your first job after school or college you'll have to get used to a whole new way of behaving pretty quickly. Since you'll probably want to make a good impression, you may feel embarrassed about making mistakes – but just about everyone does. Most people are fairly sympathetic to people who're new and are prepared to explain things and help you until you find your feet. Unfortunately there are also a few people around who can make life difficult.

On your first day make an extra effort to get to work on time. Don't leave it until the Monday morning you start before thinking about things like bus or train timetables – and don't assume you'll be able to find somewhere to park if you're driving. You'll probably have been told when and where you should report for work and the name of the person who'll tell you what to do (if not, ring the employer to find out).

It's normal for people starting a job to get shown around the place, introduced to people and have all sorts of things explained. This is the time to find out the basic things like:
■ where the loos are
■ whether there's somewhere you can eat your sandwiches if there's no canteen
■ where the first aid point is

■ whether there's a locker or cloakroom where you can leave your coat or bike helmet and so on.

You may not be able to remember everything straight away but it's best to ask your questions within the first few days, otherwise people will assume you know.

When you actually start working it's usual in most jobs for somebody to keep an eye on you, tell you what to do and explain things. If you're not sure, always ask – and don't be afraid of asking again until you're sure. If you just guess you could either get it wrong, hurt yourself or break some expensive equipment – it's not really worth it for the sake of your pride.

Timekeeping is one thing you'll learn about very quickly. In some jobs there's a mechanical clock which stamps the time you start and stop work onto a card. If you're late – even if it's only by a minute, you can lose a quarter of an hour's pay. In other places you have to sign in every morning. Even when nobody seems to take much notice about timekeeping it's best not to get into the habit of lateness – sooner or later people will start remarking on it and you could run into trouble. The same goes for taking extra-long tea breaks or lunches.

The other thing you soon find out is how to treat people. Some places are very informal while in others you have to call people by their surname. Until you've listened for a while, don't go round calling people (especially the bosses) by their first names.

Contracts

If you're employed by someone then you've got a contract. It doesn't have to be written down and you don't have to have signed anything. What the employer said when you were interviewed for the job forms part of it and in addition the law says:

■ *the employer must*: stick to any agreements about pay and conditions, not ask you to do anything illegal, look after your health and safety at work.

■ *you must*: do what the employer tells you (unless it's unreasonable or illegal), work with reasonable skill and care and give honest and faithful service.

If you're employed for more than sixteen hours a week, you're entitled to have certain things about your work in writing (part-time workers aren't and YTS trainees have their own agreements). The law says that you *must* be given a written statement of your terms and conditions of employment within thirteen weeks of starting work. This must set out:

- your hours of work (and rules about overtime)
- your job title
- how much you get paid
- how often you get paid
- what holidays you're allowed
- what to do if you're sick
- how much notice they have to give if they want to get rid of you
- how much notice you have to give if you want to leave
- what happens if you do something wrong
- who to go and see if you want to complain
- any pension arrangements.

If these things don't appear, the statement must tell you where you can find them out (they may be on a works' noticeboard for example).

If you don't get your written statement after thirteen weeks you should ask the employer for one and if nothing happens, go to the Citizens' Advice Bureau and ask for help. You should also ask advice if you're worried about the statement or don't understand bits of it. You don't have to sign the statement.

Profile

"When I accepted my new job the firm wanted me to start as soon as possible and so I handed in a month's notice at my old place straight away. The week before I was due to start though, they rang me up and said that the new offices wouldn't be ready for two weeks more. This meant that I was going to be without pay for a week – which I certainly couldn't afford. It was lucky I knew that what they had said in the interview was part of my contract – they had to pay me from the date we agreed at the start even if they couldn't give me any work."

Naaj, 19 (Projects Manageress)

Money

Although your written statement will tell you how often you're paid, don't be surprised, if it's your first job, if you don't get any money at the end of your first week or month. It's very common for workers to be paid "in hand". This means you only start getting money after the second week or month and the extra money is kept back until you leave. If you walk out of the job without giving notice you can lose this money.

This arrangement can be pretty hard on you for the first month – if you've got a bank account, try asking for an overdraft (see Chapter 5, *Managing money*). If you've been claiming supplementary benefit before you got the job you can carry on claiming up until you get paid. When you go to sign on, tell the staff at the dole office – they'll give you a form for your employer to sign.

More and more people now get their weekly wage or monthly salary in the form of a cheque or a direct debit (you have to have a bank account for this – the employer pays your money directly into the bank). Employers prefer this because it means there's less chance of money being stolen or lost. If you are paid in cash you'll probably get your money in a sealed envelope with holes in it so that you can count what you get before opening it. If you think you've not been paid enough for that week, take the sealed packed back. Only if you've not opened the envelope can you prove that you've been underpaid.

No matter whether you're paid by cash or direct debit, the law says you must get a written statement every time you're paid if you work more than sixteen hours a week (part-time workers who've been with the employer for five years or more may also be entitled to a payslip). This pay statement will tell you:

- your name, National Insurance number and any reference number the employer has for you
- your tax code (this tells the employer how much tax to take away from you)
- the date on which the payment is made
- your basic pay (what you earn in a normal working week)
- any additional pay (what you get for overtime, on commission and so on)
- the total amount you've earned that week or month (that's the basic plus any additions). This is called your *gross pay*.

Next the payslip tells you what deductions have been made from your pay. These may be:

■ income tax (there's no choice about this)
■ National Insurance contributions (you can't opt out of this either)
■ pension contributions (in some jobs you've got no choice, in others you have to agree first)
■ trade union subscriptions (you have to agree before they take this)
■ savings schemes (you have to agree to this too).

What's left of your gross pay after the deductions is your *net pay* and this is what you actually get to spend.

Some payslips also tell you how much you've earned in that job since April of that year – your *cumulative pay* and how much tax you've paid in total.

National Insurance contributions have to be paid by just about everyone over sixteen who works. Only people on very low pay don't contribute. In addition, your employer also has to pay contributions on your behalf. All this money goes to the government which uses it to pay for social security benefits and pensions. Some benefits are only available to people who've paid enough National Insurance.

Your income tax also goes to the government – but unlike National Insurance there are ways you can reduce the amount of tax you pay. Look at Chapter 5 (*Managing money*) to find out how to see if you're paying too much tax.

Always keep your pay slip in case you need to prove to the tax people or the Department of Health and Social Security what you've been paying.

Trade unions

A trade union is simply a group of workers who have joined together to protect and improve their working conditions. There are unions for people in just about every job and anyone over sixteen can join one if they want and if they can find one to accept them.

Although many employers will listen to their workers if problems come up, you've got very little power as an individual on your own. You have to rely on your employer's good nature if you want good pay and conditions – and there is always the risk of being made redundant. By organising groups of employees, unions try to balance the power of employers so that things are fairer.

What do unions do?
If you believe what you read in some newspapers, you might think that all unions do is go on strike for more money – this is a totally false picture – unions spend most of their time sitting down quietly with employers discussing and working out problems – strikes usually only happen when other things haven't worked. What unions try to do is:

- improve and protect employment conditions (pay, hours, holidays)
- improve the work environment (discussing things like heating, lighting, health and safety)
- protect their members' job security (trying to work out alternatives to redundancy)
- develop training and retraining so that people can have job satisfaction.
- protect the income of members and their families (some unions pay money to members who are out of work, retired or injured and also help the families of members who die).

On a national level, unions campaign against unemployment, work with the government and employers' organisations to plan parts of the economy and try to improve things like health and education for all working people and their families.

Joining a union
You don't have to join a union in most workplaces (though see section on *the closed shop* below) but it's usually a good idea since if you do have problems you'll need some help. If there are unions in your workplace, it's likely somebody will ask you whether you want to join. Use this opportunity to find out exactly what the union is doing and how it can benefit you. When you join, you'll usually pay a weekly or monthly subscription. The amount varies but it's usually less for workers under eighteen and for YTS trainees where the union accepts them as members (YTS trainees can join unions if eligible under their rules). Once you're a member you can go along to meetings and help decide what policies the union should follow locally and nationally. If you believe your union is getting out of touch it's important that you make sure they know what you think.

If there isn't a union in your workplace, write to the Trades Union Congress (TUC), Congress House, Great Russell Street, London WC1B 3LS. Tel: 01 636 4030. Tell them what you do and ask which union you should ask about membership. If you know of a union that sounds as if it's for people in your job, make contact directly (use the phone book or ask directory enquiries).

Some employers don't like unions and will see you as a troublemaker if you try to get anything going. You shouldn't be sacked simply for belonging, but get advice from the head office of your union as soon as any problem comes up.

The closed shop

In a few workplaces you have to join the union before you can get the job. This happens when the people already working there don't want people who aren't members to benefit from what the union does. This is common in some companies and occupations but unusual in others.

Health and safety

Wherever you work there are potential dangers, diseases and hazards. Every year millions more days are lost through industrial injuries (accidents at work) than are lost through disputes like strikes. In some industries the dangers may be very obvious:

- radiation
- chemicals
- machinery
- heat (fires, boiling water and so on)
- dust

On other occasions the danger may be less obvious, for example from:

- noise
- vibration

In addition even something as "safe" as reading can cause headaches and eye strain if lighting levels are inadequate, electrical equipment of any sort could be dangerous and there's increasing evidence that looking at computer terminals for long periods without a break is bad for you.

It's in everyone's interest to try to improve safety at work and try to reduce health risks. Employers are bound by law to try and make work and working safe and all workers have a duty in law to take care.

This means that if you're concerned about something being

dangerous you should tell your employer and your workmates so that things can be changed. In most large workplaces there's someone who's responsible for safety – you should be told who when you start working. If you have an accident (even a minor one) you should report it and make sure it gets written down in the employer's accident book.

Most accidents at work happen because people don't know the correct way of doing something, because they've forgotton or because they've been messing around. Safety's a serious matter (you could end up injuring or even killing other people – never mind yourself). What you can do is:

■ obey any rules about smoking or going into dangerous areas where you shouldn't be

■ make sure you use any protective clothing provided (goggles, gloves, boots, hats and so on)

■ always use guards and safety devices fitted to machinery – and make sure they're effective

■ don't cut corners to do things quickly at the risk of danger (if anyone tries to make you, you can refuse

■ make sure you know about the procedure if there's a fire

■ find out where first aid supplies are kept and who's responsible for them

■ never mess around in the workplace.

In addition you can learn to become safety conscious – look out for hazards and report them – don't leave safety up to the safety representatives, other people could suffer.

If you have an accident at work or fall ill because of the work you do you may be able to claim compensation (unless it was your own fault). Even if it was your fault, you may be eligible for Industrial Injury Benefit, contact the DHSS for details. If you want compensation, tell your union, they'll fight the case for you. If you're not in a union, ask the Citizens' Advice Bureau for help.

Dismissal – fair or unfair?

Dismissal means the sack. Once you've worked somewhere full-time for more than 4 weeks you can't be told to clear out immediately unless you've been caught doing something really bad – like stealing. The employer has to follow certain procedures otherwise you can claim "unfair dismissal".

Unless you think it's right that you've been fired, get advice immediately. If you're in a union, tell your shop steward or someone who runs things. If you're not, go to the Citizens' Advice Bureau or a solicitor (look in yellow pages under "s" and ask about legal aid under the Green Form scheme so you may not have to pay).

If you've worked for an employer full-time for 4 weeks or more, you have to be given at least a week's notice. If you've been there for more than two years it's more. Your written statement (see above) may mean it has to be longer than this minimum. Unless they've been with the employer for more than 5 years, part-time workers aren't protected unless it's written into their contract. The law is also different for trainees on YTS.

If you've worked for the employer for more than six months you're entitled to ask for the reasons for your dismissal to be written down and given to you within fourteen days.

If you believe that the reasons for your dismissal weren't fair you can complain to an industrial tribunal if:

■ you've been with the employer continuously for more than a year (two years for firms with less than twenty employees) unless you were sacked for trade union membership.
■ you complain within 3 months of dismissal.

To complain, you need to go to the Jobcentre, Employment Office or Unemployment Benefit Office and ask for form I.T.1, fill it in (get help for this) and send it off to one of the addresses it lists.

If you believe that the dismissal was to do with your race or sex contact the Commission for Racial Equality or the Equal Opportunities Commission (see Chapter 7, *Rights and laws*, for details).

If the tribunal which hears your case agrees with you, the employer can be made to:

■ give you your old job back as if nothing had happened
■ re-employ you (not necessarily in your old job though)
■ compensate you.

The laws concerning unfair dismissal are quite complicated, this section is only a rough guide. To find out exactly what the law says, look at the free Employment Legislation Booklets published by the Department of Employment and available from the Unemployment Benefit Office, Jobcentre or Employment Office (more details in *Help and advice*).

Time off work

Since employers aren't benefitting when you're not actually
working there aren't too many occasions when you can expect to be
paid when you're not there. Some employers are fairly generous
and won't reduce your pay if you need time off for something
urgent but don't be surprised if you do lose money. Nevertheless,
there are times when you're entitled to paid absence, some are
covered here others under later headings in this chapter. If you're on
a training scheme, things will be different.

Sickness

If you've got the written statement setting out your employment
conditions it will explain about this. Some employers run their own
schemes but there's also a basic minimum your employer must pay
you if you earn more than a certain amount. This is called Statutory
Sick Pay (SSP) and the employer gets it back from the government.
You can normally only get SSP once you've missed work for more
than three days – but there may be exception since the rules are
extremely complicated. If you aren't eligible for SSP for some
reason, or if you've been off work for more than eight weeks you
can claim state Sickness Benefit if you've paid enough National
Insurance. Again the rules are complicated so the important thing is
to check what's on your written statement and follow the procedure
your employer expects very carefully.

You can also get leaflets from the Department of Health and
Social Security (details in the phone book under "HEALTH"). Ask for
NI 244 (*Check your right to statutory sick pay*) and NI 16 (*SSP and
Sickness benefit*).

Holidays

Most full time workers have a paid holiday entitlement of at least
fifteen days (three weeks) plus public holidays like Christmas and
Easter. You may be lucky enough to have more than this. Your
written statement will explain who to tell when you want to take
your holidays. It's best to give your employer as much warning as
you can so that someone can take responsibility for the work you
would do normally. Remember, if you haven't used up your
holiday allowance at the end of a working year you can't carry it
forward into another year – don't get caught out!

Jury service
The majority of people over eighteen are eligible for jury service and if you're called the employer must allow you time off. You'll be sent details of how to make sure you don't lose money because of this.

Union activities
If your employer recognises your trade union for negotiating purposes you will usually be able to take a reasonable time off work for agreed union activities if you're one of the officials. (An example would be if you went on a course for safety representatives.) Your union's area or regional office can tell you more.

Redundancy

This occurs when you're told to leave your job because the employer is closing down, moving to a new area or reorganising the workforce. If you get made redundant then it's not your fault.

If there's a union in the workplace, the employer must consult its representatives before making anyone redundant to try and save the jobs. Only if they're unable to work anything out will people get made redundant. If you get told you're being made redundant, ask how the decision was made. If you think you were chosen unfairly (because of your race or sex for example), get advice from your union or the Citizens' Advice Bureau – you might be able to take the case to an Industrial Tribunal (see above).

If you've been working full-time for the employer for a period of two years or more without a break after the age of eighteen, you're probably entitled to redundancy money (some employers give something to all workers). The amount depends on your earnings, length of employment and age. You are also entitled to time off so that you can look for another job or arrange training. In some cases your employer may offer you a different job – if it's as good as your old one, you don't get any money if you turn it down. If the new job offered isn't as good as the old one you don't have to take it and you can get your redundancy money.

There are lots of rules covering redundancy. Always get advice. Look at the Department of Employment's booklets called *Procedure for handling redundancies* and *Facing redundancy? time off for job hunting*. They're available free from Unemployment Benefit Offices, Jobcentres and Employment Offices.

Pregnancy

Employees who are pregnant may have four rights – depending on various conditions. These are:

■ the right to time off for antenatal care with pay
■ the right to claim unfair dismissal because of pregnancy
■ the right to maternity pay
■ the right to return to work after pregnancy.

If you have to go to a clinic or to see your doctor, midwife or health visitor, your employer can't refuse to let you go and must pay you for that time. If you need to go more than once the employer can ask you for a certificate and details of your appointment. All pregnant women employees have this right – it doesn't matter how long you've been in your job or how many hours you work.

You can complain of unfair dismissal (see above) if your employer sacks you simply because you're pregnant – but you have to satisfy certain conditions first. You must have either:

■ worked continuously for your employer for at least one year, doing more than sixteen hours a week (or for five years if you only work between eight and sixteen hours).
■ *or* have worked continuously for at least *two* years if the employer has twenty or fewer workers.

The dismissal may be ruled as fair if:

■ pregnancy means you're unable to do your job properly
■ or if it's against the law to do that particular work when pregnant.

The employer must, however, try to find you alternative work before dismissing you. If you are dismissed for one of these reasons, you don't lose the right to maternity pay or to your job back if you're eligible.

If you've worked for your employer for at least two years (five if you work between eight and sixteen hours a week) and you plan to go back to work no later than six months after your baby's born, you're eligible for maternity pay. This pay is nine-tenths of your normal weekly pay, less the rate of the state maternity allowance (see Chapter 4, *Claiming benefit*) – even if you're not eligible for it. You do have to pay tax and National Insurance on maternity pay.

To get your job back after pregnancy you have to have been working for your employer for $1\frac{1}{2}$ years before you got pregnant (five years for the part-time workers mentioned above) and you

have to stay employed right up to at least eleven weeks before you
expect to give birth. (You can stay at work later than eleven weeks
before your baby's due, but you will lose maternity allowance – see
Chapter 4.) At least three weeks before you stop work, you must
write to your employer saying:

■ that you are (or will be) absent from work to have your baby
■ that you intend to come back to work afterwards
■ when you expect to give birth.

If the employer writes and asks you to confirm you plan to come
back you must reply within fourteen days – if you don't then the
employer doesn't have to keep your job for you.

   You can go back to work up to six months after you've had the
baby (though you must give your employer at least three weeks
notice of your return). If you leave it later than six months, you may
not get your job back.

   Work rights concerning pregnancy are quite complex. The
Department of Employment booklet *Employment rights for the
expectant mother* gives all the details. It's free from Unemployment
Benefit Offices, Jobcentres and Employment Offices. Look also at
Chapter 4.

Problems at work

This chapter has covered many of the most important areas where
you may find problems at work – but there are others, such as:

■ low pay
■ sexual harassment
■ racial or sexual discrimination
■ new work methods being introduced without consultation.

For all these problems, your trade union should be your first source
of help and support. If the problem is something like racism or
harassment from other workers then things may get difficult – but
don't let them get away with it, get organised.

Profile
"The person I work with simply can't accept that a woman can do
the job as well as he can. He's always trying to act superior which is
a laugh because my qualifications are in fact better than his. And
when we go to meetings he sometimes acts like he doesn't hear what
I say. At first I thought perhaps I was doing something wrong but

now I think he's pathetic. In a funny way I guess it's helped my confidence that I'm doing OK."

Nadia, 22, (Housing officer in local government)

Moving on

Sooner or later most people feel in need of a change of work. It may be because:
- the job has changed
- your interests have changed
- you think you need wider experience
- you want higher pay or status
- the people in your workplace annoy you
- you don't feel you're getting anywhere
- you made a mistake in taking the job in the first place.

If it's reached the stage where you don't think things are going to get any better where you are, start job-hunting again (see Chapter 1). Unless you can't bear it, don't leave your job until you have another set up. If you go without a good reason you may not be able to get any supplementary benefit for six weeks.

If you're not ready to let your employer know of your intentions, add a note to the bottom of application forms asking people not to contact your employer for any reference before telling you first.

When you do decide to leave it's polite to send your employer a letter saying that you wish to give notice of leaving and briefly mentioning your reasons. If you're leaving because you can't stand the place or the work, don't say so – you never know when you might need a reference, so keep it reasonably friendly. You'll also need to see your employer, to see about holidays you're owed and to fix your final leaving date.

When you go, make sure that your employer gives you a P.45. This is a form you have to give your new employer (or the dole office) which explains your tax position.

Help and advice

Organisations

Most of these will have a local office somewhere near you:
- *Department of Health and Social Security.* Details in the phone book under "HEALTH, DEPARTMENT OF". Most useful for leaflets

explaining about National Insurance. Numbers N.I.40 and
N.I.208 are particularly useful starting points.
- *Department of Employment*. Details in the phone book under
"EMPLOYMENT". Produces the detailed booklets on employment
legislation listed below (also available from Jobcentres and
Employment Offices).
- *the Careers Service*. Details in the phone book under "CAREERS".
Your local education authority careers service monitors people
during their first year at work. If you're having problems of any
sort in your first job (or training scheme), go and see them.

In addition, find out where your union's nearest office is based.

Publications
The best simple guide to the things covered in this chapter is
Workfacts for young workers, published by the Careers and
Occupational Information Centre, costing 95p plus 60p post and
packing from COIC, Moorfoot, Sheffield S1 4PQ.

Other books can be good but are often out of date. To find out
what the law is now, look at the Employment Legislation booklets
produced by the Department of Employment:
- 1. *Written statement of main terms and conditions of employment*
- 2. *Procedure for handling redundancies*
- 3. *Employee's rights on insolvency of employer*
- 4. *Employment rights for the expectant mother*
- 5. *Suspension on medical grounds under health and safety regulations*
- 6. *Facing redundancy? — time off for job hunting or to arrange training*
- 7. *Union membership rights and the closed shop*
- 8. *Itemised pay statements*
- 9. *Guarantee payments*
- 10. *Employment rights on the transfer of an undertaking*
- 11. *Rules governing continuous employment and a week's pay*
- 12. *Time off for public duties*
- 13. *Unfairly dismissed?*
- 14. *Rights on termination of employment*
- 15. *Union secret ballots*
- 16. *Redundancy payments*

3. Beating unemployment

What's happening to work? ■ no job ■
government schemes ■ creating your own job
■ new ways of working ■ help and advice

What's happening to work?

In 1972, unemployment in Britain went above one million for the
first time since the Second World War. At present:

- more than three and a quarter million people are registered
  unemployed
- almost half a million more are on government training or
  temporary work schemes
- many more women are looking for jobs but don't register
- almost 40% of unemployed people have been without a job for
  more than a year.

Within your lifetime, changes have been occurring which probably
mean that "full employment" as it existed in the 1950s and 1960s has
vanished forever. No matter which political party is in power,
there's never going to be a quick return to "normal". A lot of the old
jobs which people would do from nine to five, five days a week for
year after year have gone for good. New opportunities for work are
increasingly less like those they've replaced.

What are the changes?

In general terms, the trends are moving slowly:

- away from jobs making things towards jobs in services
- away from jobs which use muscle power towards jobs needing
  brain and finger-power
- away from jobs you can do immediately towards jobs where you
  need training first
- away from full-time permanent jobs towards part-time,
  contract or freelance jobs
- away from one career for life towards greater mobility in career
  terms.

Why have the old jobs gone?

There are all sorts of reasons why jobs have been lost – sometimes it's hard to separate different reasons but they probably include:

- *Changing technology*: More and more of the jobs which involve making things (and some office jobs too) can be done more speedily and cheaply by machines. Robots, computerised equipment and word processors can now do the work done previously by several people. New technology does create jobs too – but these often need different sorts of skills.

- *Overseas competition:* Many products can be produced more cheaply in other countries by companies which pay their workers very little. In addition, some British companies have a poor record for things like keeping to delivery dates – and find it hard to get orders.

- *Under investment:* When times were good, some British companies simply spent their profits or invested abroad rather than reinvesting in this country. This means that too many industries are now having to use inefficient or outdated equipment.

In addition, of course, different governments do have an effect on unemployment and job creation – but you should make up your own mind about which political party is most likely to help you and the country (see Chapter 8).

Finally, it's important to realise that the problem's not confined to Britain where about 12.6% of the workforce is without a job: in Spain it's more than 20%, in Belgium 18%, Ireland 16%, 17% in Holland and 12% in France. Of the richest non-communist countries only the Japanese don't have an unemployment problem.

What is going to happen?

The number of people wanting to work has been going up, the number of jobs has been going down – this means it's getting harder and harder to find paid work – even though there are lots of things which need to be done. Creating traditional jobs will help but the problem is simply too big for this solution alone. If it's no longer possible for everyone to have a job all the time, the options seem to be:

- give some people jobs all the time and leave the rest unemployed
- give everyone jobs – but only some of the time
- re-think the whole business so that "working" doesn't have to

mean working in a job for someone else and so that a job isn't the only way to get status and money.

In coming years, all three new methods will probably be tried out – along with all the old ones.

No job

If you found the last section less personal than the rest of the book, that's deliberate. The main causes of unemployment have little to do with you personally – so if you want a job and can't get one, don't think that it's your fault because it's probably not. The fact that you're out of a job is quite likely to be because of:

■ *where you live*: Unemployment isn't spread evenly throughout the UK, some regions have far more people looking for work (and even within regions there can be wide variations).

■ *your age*: About 22.5% of all unemployed people are under 25 (and that doesn't include more than 300,000 people on YTS schemes). Many employers will prefer to take on experienced workers for skilled jobs and use trainees on work experience for unskilled work in return for giving a bit of training. Older workers get a raw deal too – if you lose your job after the age of fifty, your chances of finding another are low.

■ *your qualifications and skills*: More and more jobs require higher qualifications than ever before and because there aren't enough jobs, there are often plenty of well qualified people looking. Having qualifications doesn't necessarily mean you get the job (some employers think you can be over-qualified for some jobs) but what it does mean is that the range of jobs open to you is greater.

Despite the law, you may also find that your chances are worse simply because you're black or a woman (Chapter 7 explains how to fight this sort of discrimination). Disabled people too may face prejudice and discrimination – but there's no law to fight this.

Profile

"After my firm closed down I wasn't really too worried about getting another job. I'd found my old one without much bother and I had the right qualifications for another. I thought I'd only be on the dole a couple of weeks. The first week was really good – I could have a lie-in every morning and I had a bit of money put aside. I started getting worried though after the first month and then depressed when I didn't seem to be getting anywhere. I used to just sit in front of the TV and for a while I even gave up looking for work. Now I'm working on a temporary Community Programme job – the money's not brilliant but it's got me back into the work routine and I'm starting to get interviews for permanent jobs."

Nikki, 20, (now working with disabled people in the community)

Losing a job – or not being able to find one in the first place, isn't a pleasant experience. The novelty wears off pretty quickly – as well as having to make ends meet on social security there are other pressures. Paid employment doesn't just bring in money, it also gives you:

■ status and an identity (as a secretary or mechanic or nurse for example)
■ a purpose and ambitions
■ a routine for living your life
■ contact with other people.

Take away people's jobs and they'll often lose self-respect and direction. The days often seem to run into each other with little to look forward to. Being out of work can make you feel isolated, depressed, irritable and bored — *if you let it*.

You may feel down – but you don't have to let unemployment beat you. There are ways of fighting back and one of the most important is to start to find new ways of achieving satisfaction in your life. Keep on looking for work, but think about what you really want – and how you can move towards your goals while unemployed. You may not get there but you can take a step in the right direction.

Self-help
You don't have to join a group to start building your own life outside work. Lots of things can be done on your own – but the last few years have seen the start of dozens of projects and centres for people who aren't in paid work. Some have been set up by groups of unemployed people on their own, others involve local trade unions and councils, churches, community and youth groups and workers, colleges and adult education tutors. What they all have in common is an aim to give you more strength to take control of your own life.

What groups do depends very much on what the people in them want – plus the wishes of any outside organisation that's meeting the bills. Some are especially for young people, some for older people, some for graduates. Some are for women and others for black people. It's likely that many will cover at least two or three of these areas:

- *Advice work*: Helping you to make sure you're getting the benefits to which you're entitled, explaining the system and how it works, sharing experiences and ways of staying out of debt.
- *Education and training*: The range here is enormous; a chance to brush up on your maths and spelling, to learn a language or about computers or music, providing facilities for art or videos or learning skills to help you get jobs.
- *Campaigns and politics*: Giving you the chance to make sure your councillors and MPs don't forget the unemployed, to work to improve things locally through things like free (or cheap) college courses, use of council swimming pools and so on.
- *Creating community based jobs*: Some schemes have managed to create new jobs by meeting community needs – not to make big profits.
- *Social and recreational activities*: Many places provide a place to meet for a coffee, discussion and read of the newspapers or a game of pool.
- *Job-hunting help*: Providing help with form-filling, perhaps a typewriter so you can draw up your CV, sessions where you can improve your interview techniques and learn how best to sell yourself.

Try places like local community centres or libraries to see what's going on in your area. There's also an organisation called BURN (British Unemployment Resource Network) which knows about many groups and exists to pass on information and support between them. They can give you local contacts and if there's nothing going on near you, they can give you advice to help you start a group. They also have a very good newsletter (details at end of the chapter).

There are also lots of tips about self-help activities on your own and in groups in *The Unemployment Handbook* by Guy Dauncey (details in the *Help and advice* section at the end of the chapter).

Government schemes

The Manpower Services Commission runs two schemes of special interest to unemployed people – the *Community Programme* and the *Voluntary Projects Programme*. You may also be interested in its training schemes (see Chapter 6, *Education and training*) while its help for people starting their own businesses is covered in the next section.

The Community Programme

To be eligible for this scheme you have to:

■ be receiving supplementary or unemployment benefit
■ have been unemployed for six out of the past nine months if aged between eighteen and twenty four
■ have been unemployed for twelve out of the previous fifteen months if aged twenty five or more.

In addition you have to have been out of work for the two months before you start in order to qualify. Regulations for disabled people are slightly different.

The schemes, which are organised by community groups, local councils and charities, provide temporary employment (full-time or part-time) for up to a year. Applicants work on projects of benefit to the community and are paid a weekly wage at the local rate for the job (the present average weekly pay is under £65 though). Although the programme isn't a training scheme, you may still get the opportunity of learning new skills. The sort of projects being run include:

■ decorating or insulating the homes of elderly people
■ clearing and improving derelict land
■ creating tape libraries for blind people
■ museum and archeological work
■ building BMX tracks or adventure playgrounds for local children.

Find out more about Community Programmes in your area from the Jobcentre or Employment Office. In Northern Ireland there's no Community Programme but a similar scheme called Action for Community Employment.

The Voluntary Projects Programme

This programme provides money to set up projects which help

unemployed people learn new skills and benefit the community without affecting eligibility to supplementary or unemployment benefit. You won't get paid if you take up activities under this programme but you could find out about new areas of work where you could look for jobs. Depending what projects near you offer, you could find yourself trying:

■ typing or computing
■ woodwork
■ welding
■ plastering

and using your skills to help others.

Ask at the Jobcentre or Employment Office to find out what the Voluntary Projects Programme offers in your area. VPP operates in England, Scotland and Wales but not in Northern Ireland.

Creating your own job

Not being able to find a job leads many people to think about working for themselves. Self-employment often seems an attractive idea: you're responsible for organising your life – working in your own way at times you decide and getting all the benefits of your success. Don't assume, however, that it's easy, not everyone has the skills or self-discipline to make a living for themselves and over half of all new businesses close down within their first five years. Nevertheless, self-employment is an expanding field (more than 10% of all paid workers are now self-employed) and there's more help and advice available than ever before.

Some people know (or learn very quickly) that self-employment isn't for them – but if you decide to look into it further you'll need:

■ a business idea
■ the skill and luck to make it work
■ the organisation and money to get it off the ground
■ good advice and support.

What's your idea?
You won't get very far if you just have a vague idea that it would be nice to be your own boss – you've got to know exactly what you're trying to do and be convinced that it will work. People with plenty of cash can buy into a going concern but if you're unemployed you

probably won't have enough unless, possibly, you've got redundancy money.

This means you have to start from scratch. Your idea may be to:

- use the skills in which you've trained or worked (such as typing, carpentry, hairdressing, catering, piano playing)
- expand an activity you do anyway (like repairing bikes or cars, making clothes, running a disco, writing)
- move into a gap in the market you've identified.

If you can't come up with an idea on your own, try talking to friends. Being your own boss doesn't mean you have to be on your own, you could form a partnership or maybe set up a co-operative (see below).

Here are some example of things you could do:

- typing
- driving (though make sure you're insured to use your bike or car for working)
- gardening
- modelling (try art schools and evening classes)
- photography
- second-hand dealing (records, books and so on)
- crafts (making jewellery, toys, pottery, candles, knitwear)
- picture framing
- cleaning (shops, offices or private houses)
- plumbing

Once you've worked out your idea you've got to think very hard if it's got a good chance of making money before you start to do anything. Look at what your costs will be for things like:

- premises from which to work
- stock to sell or raw material you need to produce anything
- any machines or equipment you must have
- all the administration
- your marketing or publicity.

Only if you make enough to cover all these (plus a bit to reinvest in the business) will you start making money for yourself.

This means you have to look carefully at how you're going to sell your product or service – unfortunately, a good or useful idea isn't always the same as a profitable one! Ask yourself about your customers and competitors:

- Why should people come to you rather than anyone else?
- Who is going to want your product or service?

- How much will they pay for it?
- Will there be enough demand to support you?
- What price will people pay for your service or product?
- Do your competitors charge more or less than you plan to?
- If your idea is so good, why hasn't someone thought of it earlier?

If you've managed to answer these questions without being put off there may be something in your idea.

Skills and luck

It isn't enough to have skills in providing the service or product you think will sell. You also need to be good at marketing – convincing people to come to you. This needs confidence and flair as well as a knowledge of the market place. You'll also need to have some skills in management – organisation, administration, planning and finance (especially how you'll develop the business in its early stages and where the money will come from).

If you need to learn or improve these skills, contact local colleges. Many run short part-time courses for self-employed people in things like basic book-keeping, selling, business publicity. Increasingly there are also special courses for people planning to go self-employed which outline common problems and suggest methods of overcoming them. You should also ask about training courses in self-employment at your Jobcentre or Employment Office.

You can learn these things the hard way – by having to remedy your own mistakes. You're probably spending your time more profitably though, by learning to avoid the problems in the first place.

Getting started

At a very early stage you've got to decide how your business will be organised. The options are:

- *Sole trader*: This means you simply start trading on your own. It's really simple; you can start straight away and it doesn't cost anything. The problem is that if the business fails, you are held personally responsible for any debts. This will probably not worry you if you're simply providing a service and haven't had to borrow money or get credit for stocks or equipment.
- *Partnership*: You and your partners agree what each of you will put into the business in terms of time and money and how you'll

divide up the profits. To save problems later, it's best to have this written down. The problem with partnerships is that you're still responsible for the debts if the business fails – in fact you can be held responsible for your partners' share of the debts if they can't pay.

■ *Limited companies*: This makes the business independent from you. You own shares in the company – on your own or with other people. The person or people with most shares decides how the business is run. The advantage of a limited company is that you're only held liable for any debts up to the value of the shares you own. This means you're only risking a limited amount rather than everything you own. The bad thing about limited companies are that they will cost about £200 to set up and you have to comply with other rules and regulations which mean some expense every year. Get advice from a bank, accountant or solicitor about whether your business would benefit from being a limited company.

■ *Co-operatives*: Like companies, co-ops are set up as organisations independent of the people in them. The difference is that while company shares can be held by people who don't work in them, co-ops are owned and run only by their workers (the high street co-op is a different sort – owned by its customers). Co-ops give the workers "limited liability" for debts in the same way as company shares do but they're slightly different in that people in co-ops aren't out simply to get rich quick. Co-ops are experiments in working collectively without the distinction between bosses and workers.

To find out more about co-ops, contact the Co-operative Development Agency, 20 Albert Embankment, London SE1 7TJ. Tel: 01 211 3000. There may be local agencies too. Also contact the Industrial Common Ownership Movement, 7 Corn Exchange, Leeds LS1 7BP. Tel (0532) 461737.

When you start a business it's important to stay within the law. Tell the tax people (in the phone book under "INLAND REVENUE") that you're self-employed because you'll have to pay any taxes in a different way from when you worked for someone else. Also tell the DHSS because your National Insurance position will change.

If you've been claiming supplementary or unemployment benefit, you must tell them you've been working when you go to sign on. If you don't, you risk all sorts of problems. The laws about

earning money while claiming are not straightforward – see
Chapter 4 for more details.

You'll probably need to borrow money when you start a
business. Your bank should be the starting point for this. Your bank
manager may suggest overdrafts or loans, you may also be able to
find suppliers who will give you good credit terms – but you'll
probably have to find *some* cash yourself. Think carefully before
asking family or friends for a loan.

The Enterprise Allowance Scheme
If you're claiming benefit, you may be discouraged from starting up
your own business because you can't support yourself while you're
getting set up and on your feet. In order to make things easier, the
government has set up a scheme to help. The Enterprise Allowance
Scheme pays you a weekly sum (at present £40) during your first
year of operation if:
■ you have at least £1,000 to invest in the business (this doesn't
  have to be cash – the promise of a bank loan will do)
■ you've been unemployed for at least 13 weeks
■ you can convince the people who run it that your idea is good and
  that you're capable of making it work
■ you're between the ages of eighteen and sixty five.
Ask at the Jobcentre or Employment Office for details.

Help for small businesses
The *Help and advice* section at the end of the chapter has details of
some general places you can find help and books to read but if you're
serious about self-employment there are three people you should
turn to for help at every step:
■ *A bank manager:* Help with finance to start the project and advice
  on cash flows and effective financial management.
■ *An accountant*: Guidance on keeping financial records for tax
  purposes and ensuring you have the financial information on
  which to take business decisions.
■ *A solicitor*: Assistance with taking on premises, licences you may
  need and all legal matters involved in business.

New ways of working

As the sorts of work people do changes, the ways in which work is done change too. Even though most workers will continue to be full-time, permanent employees of an organisation, the numbers of people working in different ways looks likely to rise. This may affect *when you work, for whom you work* and *what you do*.

The growth of self-employment and co-operatives (above) is one area of change but there are several more. It's quite likely that you'll use more than one of these approaches if you're looking for alternatives to traditional employment – what all the new ways have in common is flexibility and adaptability.

Changes in employment usually come about because employers find them profitable – rather than because they'll benefit workers. Even so, you may be able to create ways to work which meet your needs and give you a reasonable income.

Temporary and seasonal work

Many jobs in tourism, hotel and catering trades and harvesting only exist at certain times of the year. In lots of other work though, employers are increasingly likely to "buy in" workers when needed on a temporary basis rather than employ workers permanently in uncertain times. You may be able to find jobs because:

■ it's the right time of year
■ it's how the industry works (many jobs in building for example)
■ of holidays or sickness
■ of rush jobs which mean an extra pair of hands are needed.

If you take on these sort of jobs you may be employed by the people for whom you work, by an agency or bureau or you may be self-employed.

The advantages of working in temporary jobs are that you:

■ will get variety and a wide range of experience trying out jobs.
■ earn some money (but beware hotel jobs where you get room and board but not much cash).
■ can sometimes use this work as a way into a permanent job (if that's what you want).

It also shows prospective employers that you're fairly enterprising if you're simply trying to find an alternative to unemployment.

The big disadvantage about this way of working is, obviously, lack of security – you'll be lucky if you can move straight from one job to another, you have very little protection from the employment laws and if you fall ill you'll have to start claiming supplementary benefit. In addition the pay in some jobs isn't that high and it's not unusual in some jobs to be paid "cash in hand" – which means you could be storing up problems with tax and National Insurance in the future.

Despite the drawbacks, many people do spend a few years doing casual work – both in Britain and on the continent. If you're not tied down it's a way to see something of life. Other people do occasional temporary work (student vacation jobs being a good example).

Some ideas include:

■ tourist guide or courier work – foreign languages usually essential
■ Christmas postal work (Apply in September to your nearest main post office; you must be at least eighteen.)
■ bar tending/waiting (Ask at likely places; you have to be over eighteen to serve alcohol.)
■ kitchen and domestic work
■ work in holiday camps
■ office work (If you've got secretarial skills you can usually find some work "temping".)
■ crop picking (Raspberries in Scotland, pea-shelling in East Anglia, and many more. Some places provide accommodation but the pay's low. If you're adventurous there's the grape harvest in Europe too.)

If what you want is a working holiday, look at Chapter 11 (*Time out*).

Part-time working
The number of part-time workers has been on the increase in recent years. Traditionally, this sort of working has attracted women with family commitments but it looks as though more and more people from different backgrounds are working this way.

There are a number of disadvantages in working part-time; you may not pay enough National Insurance to claim unemployment benefit if you lose the job or get the maternity allowance, you'll have fewer rights when it comes to redundancy, sick pay, or maternity leave if you work under sixteen hours a week and you're unlikely to get any paid holidays or time off with pay. In addition, the pay and prospects in the job may be low.

Part-time work doesn't have to be all bad news though – the great thing about part-time work is that it's much more flexible. Some people choose to work part-time while they get their own business off the ground. Others combine two or more part-time jobs to get variety in their working life or widen their experience hoping to move into a job full-time. Despite the drawbacks, many part-time workers prefer it to a full-time job, saying it gives them more time to enjoy the rest of their lives.

One thing to look for when you apply for a part-time job is whether it's paid hourly or at a proportion of the full-time rate. The second arrangement is usually better for you in terms of pay and security.

Job sharing and job splitting

These are very different things. Job sharing means two people agreeing to share one full-time job so that they can have more hours to themselves. Job splitting is a government scheme which tries to get two people who both want a full-time job to make do with part-time work instead.

Job sharing is a growing trend and can be found in a surprisingly wide range of jobs at all levels. The way jobs are shared varies from place to place; sometimes one person works mornings, the other afternoons; sometimes by days (not always shared equally) and sometimes nothing's written down and the people work out what's best at particular times.

People who do share jobs like the arrangement as it gives them a combination of freedom and security of employment. Employers who can be persuaded that the extra admin is worth it usually find they benefit from having two minds for the price of one.

To find out more about job sharing, write to New Ways to Work, 347A Upper Street, London W1 0PD. Tel: 01 226 4026. They have publications (including one to help you convince an employer) and may be able to suggest ways to find a job share partner.

The Equal Opportunities Commission (details at the end of Chapter 7) also produces a free pamphlet called *Job Sharing*.

To find out more about the government's job splitting scheme, contact your local Jobcentre or Employment Office. It hasn't been very popular – since it started in 1983 only 1,000 jobs have been split but it might suit you.

Home working

You may prefer to work from home or you may have to (due to disability perhaps), either way there are probably more home-workers than you ever imagined – about one and a half million people. Many of these will be working at boring repetitive jobs like hemming clothing or packing soap but there are alternatives.

Homeworking has traditionally been very badly paid but if you've a skill to offer your prospects are brighter, examples include:

- typing (if you've a home computer you could even offer word processing)
- book-keeping
- car repairs
- hairdressing and beauty work (you can also offer a visiting service)
- childminding (you'll need to be registered with the council. Send for *So you want to be a child minder*, free from the Health Education Council, 78 Oxford Street, London WC1A 1AH for a short introduction.)

Most home workers doing these jobs will also be self-employed (see above).

Even if you can beat the low pay trap, homeworking has its disadvantages of isolation, lack of space and interruption from the other people in your home. If you're living in council accommodation there will also be problems if you're using it for work. It isn't easy to work this way, you need a lot of self-discipline to get things done but at the same time it can be a convenient and flexible arrangement if you can get it to work for you.

To find out more about the opportunities provided by new ways of working (as well as the drawbacks) look at: *How to survive unemployment* (details in *Help and advice*).

Profile

"I've never had a full-time permanent job in my life. Ever since leaving college I've made my living from a mixture of self-employment and part-time work. It wasn't that I ever planned for it to be that way but I guess I've been pretty lucky. The biggest advantage is that I'm never bored, the biggest disadvantage is the lack of security."

Alastair, 26 (writer and lecturer)

Help and advice

Places – unemployment and self-help

Contact local community centres, youth clubs, colleges and
meeting rooms to see if there are activities for unemployed people
already. Many towns will also have special centres for unemployed
people – look out for local publicity. You can also contact:

■ *BURN (British Unemployment Resource Network)*, 318 Summer
Lane, Newtown, Birmingham B19 3RL. Tel: 021 359 3562.
Information about local groups, directory of unemployment
projects (£3.20), quarterly newsletter (recommended, 50p a
time) and a start-up kit for people interested in setting up new
projects. BURN also organises conferences.

■ *Church Action with the Unemployed*, 146 Queen Victoria Street,
London EC4 4BX. Details of many new initiatives throughout
the UK.

■ *Centre for Employment Initiatives*, 140A Gloucester Mansions,
Cambridge Circus, London WC2H 8PA. Tel: 01 240 8901.
Concerned with research and information on employment
development (including new ways of working). Publishes
journal *Initiatives* (£17.50 per year) – well argued and clear,
includes ideas from overseas but quite expensive. Ask your
library to get it.

Places – self-employment

In addition to your banker, accountant and solicitor, try:

■ *Small firms centres*. Set up by the Department of Industry, these
provide information and business counselling services and give
good advice on all aspects of running small businesses.
Information and first counselling session free, extra sessions
charged for. Located in twelve main towns, dial 100 and ask the
operator for Freephone 2444 to find the nearest.

■ *CoSIRA (Council for Small Industries in Rural Areas)* offers advice
and help – including raising finance, to people thinking of
starting a business in a rural area. Get more details from
CoSIRA, Information Section, 141 Castle Street, Salisbury,
Wilts SP1 3TP. Tel: 0722 336255. or check your phone book for
details of local offices. In Scotland, contact the Highlands and
Islands Development Board, Bride House, Bank Street,
Inverness IV1 1QR. In Wales, contact the Development Board

for Rural Wales, Ladywell House, Newtown, Powys ST16 1JB
In Northern Ireland, contact the Local Enterprise Development
Unit, Lamont House, Purdy's Lane, Belfast BT8 4AR. Tel
(0232) 691031.

■ *New Ways to Work*, 347A Upper Street, London N1. Details
about job sharing.
■ *Local Co-operative Development Agencies*. Details of the national
organisations for co-ops are given in the chapter but more and
more areas are setting up local agencies. Your library will
probably be able to tell you if there's one near you.
■ *Local councils* are very helpful in many areas (particularly with
things like premises). Some have special departments to help but
if not, contact the Chief Executive's Department at your local
town hall or council offices.
■ *Local Enterprise Agencies*. Local groups often funded by councils
and existing companies to give support and advice or
information to new ventures. Exact services vary from place to
place. If your library doesn't have information about any,
contact: Business in the Community, 227A City Road, London
EC1 1JU, or Scottish Business in the Community,
22 St. Andrews Square, Edinburgh for a list.
■ To notify changes in your personal financial status, contact your
nearest offices of the Inland Revenue (tax) and Department of
Health and Social Security (National Insurance).
All the books listed on self-employment have very much more
detailed lists of contacts.

Books – unemployment and self-help
Most will also have at least a chapter on self-employment. Look at:
■ *The Unemployment Handbook* by Guy Dauncey (£2.25 from the
National Extension College, 18 Brooklands Avenue,
Cambridge CB2 2HN or from bookshops). Excellent book on
coping with unemployment, full of ideas.
■ *How to survive unemployment* by Robert Nathan and Michael
Syrett (£2.95, published by Penguin Books, from most
bookshops). Quite detailed and aimed at redundant managers.
Not quite so easy to read but worth the effort – full of tips.
■ *Nice work if you can get it* by Guy Dauncey (£1.95 from the
National Extension College, address above or from
bookshops). Looks at what's happening to work and includes

lots of examples of groups developing alternatives to
unemployment and traditional jobs. Thought provoking.

Books – self-employment

Look at:

■ *Working for yourself* by Godfrey Golzen (£5.95, published by
Kogan Page Ltd, from most bookshops). Best-selling practical
guide.

■ *The Guardian Guide to running a small business* by Clive Woodcock
(£5.95, published by Kogan Page Ltd, from most bookshops)
another good example of the many books which are available.

■ *Work for yourself* by Paddy Hall (£3.25, published by the National
Extension College, addressed above or from bookshops).
Written especially for school leavers. Lively and readable and
including case studies of people who've tried it.

4. Claiming benefit

The benefits system ■ claiming if you're out of work ■ claiming on a low income ■ maternity benefits ■ other benefits ■ appeals ■ help and advice

The benefits system

There are dozens of welfare benefits which have been created to help people in need – the problem is that they're so complicated you may not get help simply because you don't know the support to which you're entitled. The system can be a real jungle so get advice or look at one of the detailed publications mentioned in *Help and advice* – and remember, things can change. This chapter can only give the broadest of outlines.

There are some people who look on welfare benefits as charity handouts – but they're not. Whenever you're working you'll probably be paying National Insurance contributions which go towards any benefits you've claimed in the past or may claim in the future. These benefits are your *right*, so if in doubt, *claim* as soon as you can.

Benefit rates usually go up each year in November – so the exact amounts aren't given here. You can find out the figures when you need them from any office of the Department of Health and Social Security – ask for leaflet NI.196.

Types of benefit
There are basically three sorts of benefits:
- ■ *National Insurance benefits*: You get these if you, or your husband or wife has paid enough contributions when working. These benefits *aren't* "means tested" (that is, they aren't related to what you earn).
- ■ *Means tested benefits*: You don't need to have paid any National Insurance to get these – but you do have to give details of your income and circumstances.

■ *Non-contributory benefits*: There's no means test for these, you
   don't have to have paid any National Insurance – but you do have
   to meet the qualifying conditions.

When you claim, you're probably going to be more interested in
how much money you'll get rather than the rules by which you get
it. But if you do make the effort to understand the system, there'll be
less chance you'll go away without your full entitlement – because
it's a fact that you'll not get much help volunteered when you claim.
This isn't because the staff don't care, it's because there are far too
few of them and they're under incredible pressure.

Claiming if you're out of work

There are basically two main benefits paid to eligible people out of
work. These are supplementary benefit and unemployment
benefit. Lots of people get the two confused.

   You can only get *unemployment benefit* if you've been working for
an employer (not if you've been self-employed) and have paid
enough National Insurance contributions and are looking for
another job. This benefit isn't means tested and lasts for up to a year,
after which you have to claim supplementary benefit.

   Supplementary benefit can be claimed by anyone over sixteen who
isn't working full-time (see *Who can claim* below for what this
means) and doesn't have enough to live on. It's means tested – but
you don't have to have worked before to get it and you can get it
paid on top of other benefits if you qualify.

Who can claim?
You can only claim unemployment benefit if you've worked for
someone and paid National Insurance, for supplementary benefit
it's a little more complicated. Very simply, the position is:

■ if you're unemployed and available for work – YES (even if
   you're already on unemployment benefit).
■ if you're working more than 30 hours a week – NO (unless
   you've just started work, are on YTS or another government
   training scheme or are disabled).
■ if you're unemployed but less than two weeks ago were
   self-employed – NO.
■ if you're working part-time and are able and willing to take a
   full-time job – YES.

■ if you're under nineteen and in full time education – NO
(although there are some exceptions for people on their own or
parents.)

■ if you're over nineteen and in full-time education – NO (except
for degree level students who *can* claim during their vacation).

■ if you're in part-time education – YES (this must be no more
than twenty one hours of supervised study a week, less for
school leavers and people under nineteen).

■ if you've just left school – NO (you have to wait until the first
Monday in January if you leave at Christmas, the first Monday
after Easter Monday if you leave at Easter or the first Monday in
September if you leave in June.)

■ if you're not a citizen of Britain or another EEC country – NO
(although the rules here are even more complex).

There may be a few exceptions to these rules (especially if you're
disabled) and you can see already how complicated they are – if in
doubt, claim and get advice.

Remember, if you're entitled to unemployment or
supplementary benefit you'll probably also be able to claim health
benefits (see Chapter 9, *Mind and body*) and housing benefits (see
Chapter 10, *Shelter*) and possibly things like help to look for a job
elsewhere in the country (see *other benefits* below).

How to claim

First of all you should go to your local Jobcentre or Employment
Office (Careers Office if you're under eighteen) and register. This is
only compulsory for under-eighteens but it doesn't do any harm –
and you might just get lucky and find a job. If you want to claim
supplementary benefit and you're *not* unemployed see *Other benefits*
(below).

Next you should go to the nearest Unemployment Benefit Office
(find it in the phone book under "EMPLOYMENT, DEPARTMENT OF").
Here you'll be asked a few questions and told when you should next
attend to sign on. If the office is six miles or more from your home,
ask to sign on by post.

■ *If you've been working for a while*: Take along the P.45 form your
last employer should have given you or a note of your National
Insurance number. If you're eligible, your benefit will be sent to
you after about two weeks. In the meantime (or if you're not sure
if you've paid enough National Insurance) ask for form B.1 so

that you can also claim supplementary benefit. It's possible you
may get extra.

■ *If you've not worked*: You still have to claim for unemployment
benefit even though you know you won't get any (strange but
true!) before you can get a form B.1 for supplementary benefit.

Once you've got your B.1 form you have to fill it in and send it to the
nearest office of the Department of Health and Social Security
(DHSS). Ask the Unemployment Benefit Office staff where it is –
sometimes it's just next door but in some places it can be right over
the other side of town.

If you've got plenty of time and the office is close, call in and see
them, otherwise, book an appointment to see them because you can
end up waiting ages. If it's a real emergency say so – you should get
seen quicker.

When you go for your DHSS interview, take along details of:

■ any income
■ any savings (post office book, bank statements and so on)
■ your housing costs (rent book, mortgage details)
■ any hire purchase commitments.

If your claim's successful you'll be sent your Giro cheque to be
cashed at a local Post Office within a couple of weeks along with a
"Notice of Assessment" which tells you how it's been worked out.
After that you'll get another Giro every two weeks. If your claim is
successful, there'll probably be plenty of other benefits to which
you're entitled – see below.

How your supplementary benefit is worked out

The DHSS decides how much money you should get by comparing
the income you have with what they think you need in order to live.
If you've not got enough, they give you the difference. If you've got
savings above a certain level, you won't be eligible.

The way they work out your needs depends on things like:

■ your age (if you're under eighteen you get less than older people;
at the time of writing there are rumours that the government
may stop most people under eighteen claiming altogether – to
encourage people to go on YTS. Watch out!)
■ your children (you get more money for each child)
■ any special needs (such as certain medical diets, or if your home's
very difficult to heat and so on)
■ your circumstances (you get more if you're living in your own

home or renting than you do if you live in your family home or are in care).

Possible problems

If you're turned down for unemployment benefit it may be because the benefit staff think you left your last job without any reason – you can be denied benefit for six week if this is the case. If you're sacked you can claim immediately so the moral seems to be "don't walk out of a job you hate, get yourself fired if you can do without the reference".

If you're turned down for supplementary benefit it may be because they think you're living with someone "as husband and wife" (whether you're married or not) and they think that person should be supporting you. This is an area where the rules can get very complicated – look at the *National Welfare Benefits Handbook* (see *Help and advice* below) for the simplest explanation of the rules about this but also remember you'll *probably* have problems if:

■ you're living in the same household
■ you're in a stable relationship
■ you're having a sexual relationship with the person
■ you're sharing expenses with the person
■ you and the other person are parents of a child
■ you appear in public as wife and husband.

If you have problems in these, or any other areas, appeal and get help.

Single payments

These are special payments to help you with expenses which can't be paid for out of your normal benefit. You won't get them simply to pay for large bills like gas or electricity. Single payments are difficult to get so find detailed help.

Working and claiming benefit

There are ways in which you can earn a bit of money to supplement your unemployment or supplementary benefit – but if you don't know the rules you could end up in serious trouble.

Unemployment benefit is generally not paid for a Sunday – this means that you can usually earn money without it affecting your benefit if you work on Sunday. You must tell the Unemployment Benefit Office about this work each time you claim if you're to stay out of trouble.

People on unemployment benefit can also earn money during the week without it affecting their benefit if it's less than £2 a day (watch out for changes to this figure), if you're still available for full-time work and if it's not work in your usual occupation (if you're working for an employer).

If you're getting supplementary benefit, any income you get after the first £4 a week and after expenses will mean a cut in your benefit. You should always declare *any* work you've done otherwise they might think you're not really available for work and stop your benefit altogether.

If you're doing voluntary work there are special rules – ask at the DHSS Office for leaflet NI.240 called *Voluntary work and social security benefits*.

Claiming on a low income

You can claim supplementary benefit if you're on a low income and can't make ends meet – but you don't have to go through the procedures which unemployed people do. You can either write to the DHSS saying you want to claim or you can get form SB.1 to fill in from any Post Office or DHSS office, there's no need to go to the Jobcentre or Unemployment Benefit Office but otherwise your claim is handled in the same way.

If you're in full-time work and bringing up children on low wages, you may be entitled to family income supplement. What you get depends on your earnings and the number of children you have. This benefit is entirely separate from child allowance (see below). In order to claim, ask for form FIS.1 at your Post Office or local DHSS office.

Remember, if you're claiming either of these benefits you'll probably be entitled to others too – see below.

Maternity benefits

If you're expecting a baby there are a number of benefits to which you may be entitled. These include:

■ *Maternity allowance*: To get this you have to have been working and paying sufficient National Insurance. It's money you can get for up to eighteen weeks, starting eleven weeks before your baby's due. This benefit isn't means tested.

■ *Maternity grant*: This is a one-off payment which virtually all mothers without exception can claim for help towards the costs of having a baby. It's not a lot (only £25 per baby at the time of writing) but it's worth getting.

■ *Health benefits*: Just about every pregnant woman and woman who's had a baby in the last year can get free prescriptions and dental treatment. If you're getting supplementary benefit or family income supplement you'll also be able to get free milk and vitamins until your child is five years old. A few other people who're not getting these benefits may also be able to claim free milk and vitamins too.

■ *Supplementary benefit single payments*: If you're claiming supplementary benefit and you're expecting a baby or have just had one you may be able to get lump-sum payments for the things your baby needs. It's probably best to get advice here so that you can make the most of your entitlement.

■ *Maternity leave*: To get paid maternity leave you have to have been working for your employer for at least two years – look at Chapter 2, *Working for a wage* for more details.

Look at the section *Help and advice* for details of how to claim and leaflets with more information.

Other benefits

If you're on a low income or aren't in paid work there may be other benefits you can claim. Many of these will be from the DHSS but a few will be from other sources like your local council or the Manpower Services Commission. One of the most useful guides to these is called *Which Benefit* and is available free from DHSS offices (ask for FB.2). It's a brief description of the main benefits available from all sorts of sources and gives you details of places to find out more information and the right leaflets to ask for.

Some of the common areas for which you may get help are:

■ *Children*: Just about everyone who's responsible for a child under sixteen can get child benefit – a tax-free weekly payment of just under £7 a week. If you're a single parent, bringing up a child on your own you can get an extra payment for your first or only child (at present just over £4 a week). Neither of these benefits are means tested and you don't have to have paid National Insurance to get them.

Remember too that you shouldn't have to pay anything for the

health care of any children you have. You should also claim free
school meals and free school milk for your children if you're on
supplementary benefit or family income supplement (not many
areas provide free milk however). For these benefits, ask your
children's Headteacher for details of the Educational Welfare
Office.

■ *Disability*: If you have a disability, all sorts of special regulations
come into force concerning your benefit entitlement, eligibility
for supplementary benefit is relaxed, you may qualify for an
attendance allowance or/and a mobility allowance from the
DHSS. Your local council may be able to arrange things like
special aids or home adaptations, bus passes, home helps and so
on. Contact them for details. The Manpower Services
Commission allows people with disabilities onto its training
courses without you having to satisfy the usual eligibility rules as
well as running special schemes to help your employment
prospects. See also Chapter 9.

■ *Illness and injury*: If you're normally at work you will usually be
able to get Statutory Sick Pay and if you've paid enough
National Insurance, you'll probably be entitled to sickness
benefit instead or as well as this. If you're injured at work there
are a number of benefits for which you may qualify. Get help
from your Trade Union or Citizens' Advice Bureau.

■ *Single parents*: In addition to the special regulations affecting
family income supplement and supplementary benefit if you're a
single parent, you may also be able to get additional tax
allowances. Ask for leaflet IR.29 from your local Inland Revenue
office. Remember that you can get one-parent benefit in
addition to any child allowance you claim – and that these
benefits don't depend on your income.

■ *Changing your job*: The Manpower Services Commission runs
three different schemes to help people look for (and start) jobs in
new areas of the country. The regulations are rather strict and
you should check the rules *before* you go off for any interviews.
Ask about the Labour Mobility Schemes at your nearest
Jobcentre or Employment Office.

■ *Housing*: If you're on supplementary benefit, the DHSS will help
you apply to your local council for housing benefit (see Chapter
10, *Shelter*) but you may also qualify for the sorts of reasons
above or others. Ask your local councils about help.

There are other benefits not mentioned here for which you may qualify. Contact the Citizens' Advice Bureau if you want to find out your rights in full.

Appeals

If you're refused benefit when you're sure you should be getting it or if your benefit is suddenly reduced or cut off without good reason, you can challenge the decision. There are two ways of doing this: *a review* or *an appeal*.

You should ask for a review if there:
■ has been a mistake about what the law says
■ are facts that the benefit officer got wrong or did not know about.
You can ask for a review at any time and it's usually quicker and simpler than a full-scale appeal – although if your request for a review is refused, you'll have to appeal. It's usually best to ask for a review by writing to the DHSS office although you could phone if it's urgent.

You are allowed to appeal against any decision which a benefit officer takes (but watch out for "decisions taken in the name of the Secretary of State" because there's nothing you can do about these). What you must do is write to the benefit office within four weeks of the decision being made saying "I want to appeal" and giving details of the decision about which you disagree. You don't have to say any more than this but if you do set out exactly what you're asking for and why you think it's your entitlement it may mean they change their minds straight away. Remember to include all relevant information if your appeal is on the grounds of hardship or special circumstances.

It will usually take about five weeks for your appeal to be heard (but if your need is urgent, explain this when you write and then keep contacting the Appeals Officer at the DHSS until you get a date for your hearing).

When you go to the National Insurance Local Tribunal for your appeal to be heard, you should take someone with you to help you put your case – it's your right and can often help.

Your case will be heard by a lawyer (who chairs the proceedings), someone put forward by the local trades council and someone appointed by the government. Tribunals aren't like courts – they're not as formal but you may still get a bit nervous, that's why it's good to have someone (and it can be anyone) with you.

Use the time before your hearing to get advice on how to prepare your case. Ask the Citizens' Advice Bureau and look carefully at the books in *Help and advice* below. Make notes to help you.

Help and advice

Books
The best guides to the benefits system are published by the Child Poverty Action Group, a national charity. For detailed and relatively clear information on supplementary benefit, family income supplement, housing benefit and other means tested benefits, look at *The National Welfare Rights Handbook* (price £3.50, new edition every year from bookshops or CPAG, 1 Macklin Street, London WC2B 5NH. Tel: 01 242 3225.)

The Guide to Non-Means Tested Social Security Benefits (price £3.50, available from the same sources as above each year) covers other National Insurance benefits like unemployment benefit. Many libraries will have copies – but make sure you look at an up to date edition.

The government also publishes its own guide, the *Supplementary Benefits Handbook* – not quite as helpful but worth looking out for in your library.

Leaflets
There are dozens and dozens of DHSS leaflets. Some are available from larger Post Offices but you should be able to get any from their local offices. Some are very complicated but others have been rewritten in a much clearer style. The most common ones are:

■ FB.2 *Which Benefit?* – brief guide to what's available, good starting point.
■ FB.20 *Leaving School* – very clear pocket guide to the whole social security system.
■ FB.23 *Going to college or university* – explanation of your National Insurance position.
■ FB.8 *Babies and benefits* – guide for expectant and new mothers.
■ FB.9 *Unemployed* – *help you can get to make ends meet.*

In addition to these guides which tell you which specialist leaflets you should get (and from where) ask for leaflet NI.196 which gives you the up to date rates of benefit.

All these leaflets are free.

Organisations
Always try DHSS and Unemployment Benefit Offices for help – but don't expect much because the staff are usually overworked and under a lot of strain. The DHSS are presently experimenting with Freefone services so you can ring up with your benefit problems. Dial 100 and ask for *Freefone DHSS* – if it's operating in your area you should get put through.

Use your Citizens' Advice Bureau for help with detailed queries, also any Law Centres, Neighbourhood Centres or Welfare Rights Projects in your area. Centres for the Unemployed will usually be able to help and so will many youth workers if you ask. If you want to pass on any tips or experience to others, why not join or try and start a Claimants Union group? These are self-help groups of claimants who try to assist each other through the maze of regulations.

5. Managing money

Budgeting ■ banking ■ saving ■ borrowing
and credit ■ buying ■ consumer rights ■ tax ■
help and advice

For most of us, the main problem with money is that we don't ever
seem to have enough of it! Housing, transport, clothes and food as
well as luxuries like records, films or drink seem to soak up the cash
before we know it. Whether your income comes from a job or a
training allowance or from social security benefits, it's likely that
making ends meet will be a problem to a greater or lesser extent.

This chapter can't teach you how to get rich overnight
(unfortunately), but it does suggest ways you can make your
money stretch further and get good value for it.

Budgeting

This is all about organising your finances and may seem really
boring – but it's worth doing since the lower your income, the more
benefit you can gain from knowing where your money's going and
planning your cash needs in advance.

If you can't budget, you'll not be able to afford things like
holidays away from home without creating all sorts of problems for
yourself. It can be pretty frightening to be faced with a large bill you
can't pay; some people will try to ignore it but the problem won't go
away, it'll just get worse. Budgeting may mean you'll have to go
without things sometimes but it can help you avoid financial
disasters.

What you've got to do is make a list of all your income over the
next week or month. This can be your:
■ wages or salary (after tax and National Insurance)
■ training allowance
■ student grant.
Next you've got to monitor your spending and try to work out
your likely outgoings over the same period. This will include:

64

- *regular lump-sum spending*: Rent, fares to work, electricity bills, gas, telephone, TV licence, motor insurance.
- *irregular lump sums*: Clothes, repairs, presents, holidays, parking tickets.
- *everyday spending*: Food, petrol, papers and magazines, entertainment, cosmetics, books.

Some things you may not be able to monitor accurately (telephone bills, car repairs) but you should try and make a realistic estimate of weekly or monthly costs – and remember that your heating bills will be higher in winter. With other things (like your TV licence or motor insurance) you can look at what you pay and divide it into weekly or monthly amounts.

Add up all your spending and then compare the total with your income.

- *If your income is higher than the level of your spending*: Congratulations! You're obviously pretty good at budgeting already and will be able to save the extra for emergencies or for when you want luxuries – so long as you've not forgotten anything (holidays perhaps?)
- *If your income and expenditure match*: You're OK as long as you've planned in some savings. If not, think how you'd cope if something unpredictable happened.
- *If your spending is higher than your income*: You'll either have to increase your income (a spare time job perhaps) or cut your spending – and the sooner you can do so, the less painful it'll be.

Look at each of your expenditure headings and work out how to cut costs.

- Accommodation is likely to be the largest figure on your list. If it's making up more than one-third of your income perhaps you should think about taking somewhere smaller.
- Regular bills like electricity or gas and the phone will also figure quite high on your list. You won't be able to avoid expenditure like this but you can be cost-conscious (saving your phone-calls until the cheap rate period where possible for instance). If you find it hard to save for these bills, saving stamps may make things easier. Ask about ways to spread the cost at your Post Office or at gas or electricity showrooms.
- Travel costs are usually fairly expensive – but if they're necessary to get you to and from work then all you can do is make sure that you buy a travelpass or season ticket for the longest period you

can afford since these will almost always work out cheaper.
Alternatively think about buying a bike or seeing if you could
walk some (or all) of the way to work in good weather.

■ You aren't going to be able to do without food but it's not hard
to cut the costs by shopping around and doing without some of
the most expensive dishes – what's more, once you start
thinking more carefully about what you eat it's likely that your
diet will improve as well. One way to cut costs is to take your
own lunch to work rather than eating out. If your employer
provides a free or subsidised canteen then do the opposite though
– make lunch your main meal and just have a snack in the
evening.

■ Drink and tobacco are two areas where you should be able to cut
down your spending. If you can cut out regular lunchtime
sessions at the pub you'll save money and probably feel better
too, if you can stop smoking entirely you'll be healthier and
probably have a few pounds extra each week.

Profile

"Every term when I get my grant I always promise myself to plan
my spending. I allocate a certain amount for entertainment, some
for clothes and so on. Things never seem to work out though and
I'm invariably in debt by the time vacation comes round. When I
start to overspend my targets I always say to myself that I'll make it
up next week – particularly for things like clothes, but somehow I
never do."

Michelle, 20 (Student)

Banking

You don't have to have a lot of money to open a bank account and
unless you're having to live on social security benefit, you'll
probably find one useful. Some employers don't like to give out
wage packets (there's a lot more chance that it'll all get stolen) so
instead they like to give you a cheque or pay the money directly into
the bank accounts of their employees. You'll find an account helpful
too: it means you don't have to carry lots of cash around and risk
losing it, it means your money's safe and it can help you save.

Choosing a bank

It can be hard to see how one bank's any different from another – but there are some ways. You should shop around to see which one offers the best deal for you and which is convenient. There are four main banks:

- Barclays
- Lloyds
- Midland
- National Westminster

In addition there are others:

- Co-operative Bank
- Clydesdale Bank
- Royal Bank of Scotland
- Trustee Savings Bank
- Williams and Glyns Bank
- Yorkshire Bank

and the Post Office also offers most banking services through its National Girobank. The sorts of questions you should ask are:

- will the bank make any charges for looking after your money? (if so, how are they worked out and how much are they?).
- will the bank pay you any money for looking after your account (the Co-op bank does)?
- are there any perks for students, school leavers or people in their first job? (Lots give free banking plus a range of other goodies.)
- does that branch (or any other) open on Saturdays? (Normal banking hours are 9.30 to 3.30, Monday to Friday only.)

Shop around for the best combination for your needs.

You can find out simply by walking in and telling the cashier that you're thinking of opening an account and would like to ask a few questions first. They'll usually be very helpful since they're keen to get their hands on your cash (even if it's not much now, it may be in the future)!

Opening an account

You only need a minimum of £1 and a reference from someone who's already got an account in order to open your own. There are two main types:

- current accounts
- deposit accounts.

The first of these is for money you need to use on a day to day basis, the second is for savings and is explained in that section below.

Before you can take money out of your account you've got to put some in. There are special forms for this (ask the bank how to fill them in when you open the account) so you can pay in any cash or cheques that you get. In addition if you tell your employer your account number and bank branch, you may be able to get your wages or salary paid in directly.

If you *do* open your account with just £1 the bank may delay giving you a cheque book but otherwise you're given one which allows you to get your money from the bank easily and to pay other people for things instead of using cash. When you write a cheque to someone you put their name on the top line, when you want to withdraw some money for yourself you write "Cash" on the top line.

If all you've got is your cheque book then you won't be able to make the best use of your bank account. People may not be happy about taking your cheques unless they know you since they can't tell whether there's enough money in your account to pay them. Even other branches of your own bank won't cash your cheques without first making a phone call (for which they charge you about 50p!) to check you're OK unless you've made an arrangement with them.

What you need is a cheque card which acts as a guarantee from your bank that it will pay all cheques you write that are under £50. If you've got a cheque card you can also get cash from *any bank* (not just your own) up to a maximum of £50 a day although you may be charged by other banks for this service.

The bank doesn't have to give you a cheque card. Sometimes they make you wait 6 months to see if they can trust you, otherwise they might give you one as soon as your grant cheque or first wages get paid in. If you're under eighteen they may be reluctant but if a parent banks at the same place, ask them to have a word with the manager.

If you've got a cheque card it isn't hard to write cheques for money you don't have. This is not the way to run your account – banks hate people who do this without making special arrangement (see *Borrowing* below) and you can get into all sorts of trouble – with the bank and with the people you gave the cheque to.

If you do get overdrawn (or for some banks only, if your balance falls below a certain limit which varies from bank to bank) you have to pay charges – often for the next three months. If this happens, cut down the number of transactions you make (payings in or takings out) because this affects the amount.

Other bank services

You will be sent a statement every month or so which records what withdrawals have been made and also what's been paid into your account. You can check this with your own records to make sure you know your exact financial position.

Your bank may let you have a cash card which allows you to withdraw money from banks with wall cash dispensers outside normal hours (very useful if you can't get to a bank during working time).

If asked, the bank will also make regular payments for you without you having to write a cheque. Get them to explain to you about Standing Orders and Direct Debits.

If you ever lose your cheque book, cheque card or cash card or have them stolen, inform the bank *immediately* so that you're not held responsible for paying if someone misuses them.

All the banks produce plenty of glossy leaflets explaining the many services they provide – go and pick some up if you want to find out more.

Saving

If you can manage to save money, don't just leave it in a drawer at home, don't even keep it in your current account in the bank – use it to make you some money (no, not in a betting shop!). You should only have as much money in your wallet, purse or current account as you need over the next week or month – use any extra to earn interest. There are a number of places you can save:

Building societies
If you're paying income tax these will probably be your best bets. Building societies like the Halifax, Abbey National and many others use the money people save to make loans to people to buy houses (see Chapter 10 *Shelter*). In order to attract your money they pay interest and the tax you have to pay on this is taken away by them. They run a variety of schemes with differing rates of interest depending on how much money you invest, how long you promise to leave it with them and whether you're investing regularly or not. Building societies are open longer hours than banks and some are starting to offer cheque books and cash dispensers just like banks in order to attract your money. In addition, if you ever want to buy your own home, you're more likely to get a mortgage from a building society if you've been saving with them.

Get details of the various schemes from a number of building societies before you invest. See who offers the best deal.

Bank deposit accounts

These are bank accounts which do pay you interest but don't normally give you a cheque book (there are a few exceptions). You often have to give them seven days notice before you take the money out and any interest you earn is liable to tax.

National Savings Bank

This is a scheme run for the government by the Post Office. You can pay in money at most Post Offices and can withdraw small amounts on demand, larger sums with notice. As well as Savings Accounts where the interest is low but (up to a limit) tax free, National Savings also runs Investment Accounts with high interest. You have to pay tax on this but if you're not working it's probably the best deal around.

   Look out for leaflets on National Savings at most Post Offices. For longer term investments, there are also National Savings Certificates.

Borrowing and credit

This is about getting money and paying it back later or buying something and being given time to pay for it. Either way it'll probably cost you extra since not only will you have to repay the loan or pay for what you've bought but you'll also have to pay interest. The only exceptions are if you can:

■ borrow from family or friends who won't charge you. (If you do this make sure you pay back promptly or you'll cause very bad feeling.)
■ find shops which offer interest-free credit.
■ use a credit card and pay off the bill in full promptly.

The various ways of borrowing cost different amounts so always compare methods and go for the cheapest. If you're under eighteen, you usually won't be able to borrow unless you have an adult guarantor who'll pay your debt if you can't.

Credit cards

Credit cards linked to particular banks can be the cheapest way of buying things on credit. Access and Visa cards allow you to buy goods and services from places showing the card sign up to a certain limit. Each month you get sent a statement from the credit card company which tells you how much you owe and tells you what you have to repay. If you repay the whole amount owed immediately there's no interest – so you've had a month's interest free credit. If you only repay part of your bill you're charged interest on what's left. The advantages of these cards are that they are convenient, widely accepted and can allow you free credit. The disadvantages are that you can get tempted into buying more than you can repay at once and end up paying interest which soon adds up.

You can also borrow cash with your credit card – but you start paying interest on what you've borrowed immediately, there's no free period. If you've got two cards (Access and Visa) it is possible to juggle money between them – look at the magazine *Which* for December 1982 for details (larger libraries should have it on file).

To get your own credit card you have to be over eighteen. If you're younger, you could try to get a card for someone else's account (if they let you). You don't *have* to have a bank account but it's unlikely you'll get one if you don't. Forms are available from banks.

If you lose your card, tell the company immediately as well as the police.

There are other cards (like American Express) which work in a different way – these are charge cards, but since it costs you money to even get one of these cards, you'll probably not want to bother with them unless you're on a high income.

Shop accounts
Many chain stores operate their own card accounts. There are various types:
- monthly accounts
- budget accounts
- option accounts.

It won't cost you anything to open an account but the way you pay off what you spend can vary. With monthly accounts you usually have to pay off everything you owe within two or three weeks of getting their statement – but you do get a few weeks interest free credit. With budget accounts you make regular monthly payments whether you buy anything or not and you have to pay interest on any money you owe. Option accounts work rather like credit cards – you either pay off everything you owe when they send you a statement or just a bit and get charged interest on the remainder.

Sometimes shop accounts can work out fairly expensive – look at the section on comparing the cost of credit below to make sure it's a good deal. You will usually have to be over eighteen to get a card – look out for leaflets in major stores to tell you more.

Hire purchase (HP)

It's possible to buy some expensive goods under HP schemes arranged by shops. This involves signing an agreement to pay a deposit on goods and then a number of monthly repayments over a year or more. Although popular, this sort of credit has two main drawbacks:

■ it can work out very expensive as interest rates are quite high.

■ the goods don't belong to you until you've paid the final instalment. This means they can be taken back if you fall behind with the payments and *you* can't sell them until they're yours. (Watch out when buying secondhand that the goods aren't being bought by the "seller" on HP.)

You won't be able to make HP agreements if you're under eighteen.

Overdrafts

If you have a bank account then you can ask the manager if you can write cheques for more money than you have in your account (up to an agreed limit). The bank doesn't have to agree to let you have an overdraft – and if you do it without asking first they aren't very pleased. Although you'll get charged interest if you can arrange an overdraft, this will usually be one of the cheapest ways of borrowing money. If you need the extra cash for a period longer than just a few weeks the bank may suggest you take out a loan.

Bank loans

You don't have to have an account with a bank to ask for a loan (though it'll usually help). Loans are normally arranged to pay for large items like cars, furniture, even holidays. To get one you may not even have to see the bank manager – just fill in a form which asks the reason you want the money, how much and for how long (the longer you take to repay a loan, the more expensive it gets). So long as the bank thinks you're able to meet the repayments, you're quite likely to get your loan – after all, loans are how the banks make their money. The interest you pay will be more than that for an overdraft but probably cheaper than anywhere else.

Money lenders

If you can possibly help it, avoid money lenders and finance companies since they charge higher interest rates than just about anyone else. If you have to use a money lender always make sure he or she is licenced. Try to get any agreements checked by a Consumer Advice Centre (see *Help and advice*) before you sign. *Always* find out the APR (see *Comparing credit* below) when using a money lender. Money lenders won't give you a loan if you're under eighteen.

Pawnbrokers

An old-fashioned way of borrowing money for short periods. You can get a loan by giving goods (usually jewellery) as security. You also pay interest. The pawnbroker can sell the goods if you haven't repaid the loan and interest within a set period. You *don't* have to be eighteen to pawn something.

Comparing credit

There is a way to compare the costs of different ways of borrowing – through the *Annual Percentage Rate* (APR). The law says that anyone lending money must calculate their interest rates in the same way. The higher the APR, the more expensive the loan or credit arrangement. By the law the APR expresses the *total* charge – including any administration fees or insurance you have to pay.

Always shop around – and remember that the cheapest way to buy anything is usually to save up the money first! (If you ask, you may even be able to get a discount for paying cash there and then.)

If you're refused credit

No-one *has* to give you credit or a loan – and they don't have to tell you why not – but sometimes it's because they've been given information on you by an agency and don't think you're a good risk. You can ask for details of any agency which has provided information on you. If you apply in writing within twenty eight days of being refused and the amount is under £5,000 you have the right to be told. If you write to the agency with a fee of 25p. they have to send you a copy of your credit file – and if anything on it is wrong, you can insist it's changed (get help from a Citizens' Advice Bureau or one of the other agencies listed in *Help and advice*).

Buying

If you wait long enough and try hard enough you will often be able to avoid paying the full price on all sorts of goods or services. Here are a few ideas:

Discounts
■ *Ask for cash discounts*: If you've got the nerve this can get good results for expensive items. (Since shops have to pay commission to Access and Visa each time you use your credit card, you can quite often get about 5% off for offering cash instead. Less likely to work in chain stores.)
■ *Ask about student discounts*: The National Union of Students runs a discount scheme but any student union card may work and get a 5–10% reduction.
■ *Try for trade discounts*: If you've got business cards or use an order book (available from stationers) you may sometimes be able to get substantial trade discounts from wholesalers.
■ *Use friends for staff discounts*: Staff in shops and manufacturers are often allowed to buy at trade prices – get them to buy things for you.
■ *Discount travel*: see Chapter 11.

Cheap buying
■ *Buy from markets*: Quite a few markets aren't really much cheaper than shops (and you're less likely to be able to exchange goods or get refunds since you'll probably not get a receipt) but try looking out for bargains in fruit and veg from about 3pm, especially on Saturdays. (Some supermarkets also mark down meat and cheese on its "sell by" date.)
■ *Buy in bulk*: Get together with friends or flatmates and you should be able to save money on plenty of things – from food to household goods like washing powder or loo rolls. Check out local traders to see if they'll give extra discounts for really big buys or see if you can get a cash and carry card from a wholesaler (some will only deal with shops though).

■ *Buy in sales*: First of all check that it's a real bargain before you decide to buy anything – some of the goods aren't reduced at all but are "special purchases" bought in simply for the sale. Check also that the goods aren't in the sale simply because they're damaged – although these *can* be very good value. It's easy to get carried away in sales and buy things because they're cheap and not because you really want them. However, sales can be very good, particularly for major purchases – Hi-fi for example and also for ordinary things like shoes.

■ *Buy secondhand*: If you're prepared to hunt around a lot of old rubbish you may be able to uncover some excellent buys – especially with furniture and sometimes clothes as well. Be more careful about buying electrical goods – which could be dangerous as well as faulty. Most people of course, buy their first (and second, third and fourth!) car secondhand – see also auctions. If you're in a motoring organization, they'll usually check over a car for you for a small fee. Remember, you can't expect secondhand goods to be of the same quality as new ones.

■ *Look out for offers*: Whether it's free rail tickets with your washing powder or trial subscriptions to magazines offers can be a good way of getting things cheap or free (anyone who buys coffee or washing powder full price needn't – just look for the coupons in your local paper or coming through the door!). Even so, always compare the cost of the shop's "own brand" which may be even cheaper – and possibly made by the same manufacturer.

■ *Colleges*: If any of your local colleges has a hairdressing or catering department, there are often plenty of good deals going – ask. Most large hairdressers will also have a cheap night for "models" so their trainees can practise.

■ *Buying at auctions*: You can get all sorts of useful household stuff and furniture from auctions. It's not just antiques and posh things. There's usually a viewing day a couple of days beforehand so you can look over what's there. Watch out for faulty goods – you won't normally be able to take them back. Work out beforehand what you want to pay and *don't* go above it, remember too that there may be a buyers's commission to pay. Look up your local auctioneers in the yellow pages. You can pick up cars really cheaply at auctions – but you won't be allowed a test drive and may only be allowed the briefest and most simple inspection, so be careful.

One magazine is entirely about "best buys", it's called *Which?* and is published by the Consumers Association. You can't get it in newsagents but try your library. They also have trial subscription offers for three months quite regularly – look out for adverts or write to the Consumers Association (details in *Help and advice*).

Consumer rights

There are a whole number of laws which give you some protection against sharp practices and also a number of organisations which can offer help.

Complaining

If you're not satisfied with a service or with goods you've bought or hired, don't shrug it off, complain! If you know your rights you may be able to get something done about it.

Return goods with which you're not satisfied to the shop where you bought them. Take along any receipts or packaging that proves where they were bought. Ignore any notices the shop has about not accepting responsibility or not giving refunds (even for things bought in sales) – they're probably not valid in legal terms. Explain why you're not satisfied. Under the 1979 Sale of Goods Act the shop or trader has to put things right if what you bought was not:

■ of "merchantable quality" (this means, for example, that a pair of jeans should have both legs the same length, shoes should have soles and so on).

■ fit for its purpose (for instance, a cassette player should be able to play your cassettes and an alarm clock should have an alarm).

■ accurately described (so a cotton shirt, for example, shouldn't be made out of nylon).

The shop or trader *doesn't* have to put things right however if you
■ didn't buy the goods yourself
■ damaged the goods
■ knew or could easily have seen that the goods were damaged anyway
■ simply got home and changed your mind about wanting the goods.

If you're in the right, you should be able to get your money back unless you've had the goods some time before they became faulty or you waited before taking them back, or the fault's only small. In these cases, the shop may offer you a replacement or repair. Get advice if you're not happy with this. The shop may also offer you a credit note rather than cash – but you don't have to accept this if you want cash. If you *do* decide to take a credit note, ask whether or not there's a time limit in which you should use it. Don't let traders pass the buck by saying you've got to take up your complaint with the manufacturer – it's their responsibility.

If you buy something secondhand, you can't expect it to be as good as new but you will have the same rights unless you bought it privately (see below). When you buy from auctions you have fewer rights.

There are other laws which concern traders who sell you short weight or measure and those who sell dirty, bad or impure food and drink. If you have problems with these, don't let traders off if they say it was a mistake – you should contact your local Trading Standards Officer and Environmental Health Officer (sometimes called Consumer Protection Officers or Public Health Officers). Get their addresses from the phone book – look under the name of your local council. You should also contact Trading Standards Officers if a trader says or writes something untrue about a product.

When you buy something privately from an individual you don't have so many rights – only that the goods should be accurately described, so watch out when buying things like cars. It's usually best to get someone to come with you who can help you check goods are working and good value if you're thinking of buying something this way.

If you live in England, Wales or Northern Ireland (but not Scotland) there's an additional law; the 1983 Supply of Goods and Services Act which gives you the same sort of protection if you're hiring goods or getting them in part exchange – ask for advice as to how the law works.

Complaining about services
It's more difficult to interpret the law when it comes to the supply of services – so it's best to get advice from one of the organisations mentioned in *Help and advice*. What you can usually expect when someone carries out a service like fixing your car, cutting your hair or dry cleaning your clothes is that:

- they do the job as agreed (so if you ask for your hair to be dyed blue and they do it green, it's not as agreed).
- they do it for the agreed price. Remember though that an *estimate* isn't the same as a *quotation* for a service. (A quotation is a fixed price for the service and is part of your contract with the person providing it, an estimate could be more or less than the price – it's just a rough guideline.)
- it's done to a reasonable standard, with reasonable care and with suitable materials. (This means that if your plumber tries to plug a leak with chewing gum you'd probably be able to get your money back.)

Support

If you complain and don't seem to be getting anywhere with the person who provided the goods or services, ask for help from the Citizens' Advice Bureau, Consumer Advice Centre (some areas only) or Trading Standards Officer.

Tax

Unless you're only earning a fairly small amount each year you'll be liable for income tax. This is money that goes to the government to pay for things like defence, police, courts, roads, education, health services, welfare benefits and so on.

The amount you pay depends on what you earn during a tax year (which starts on April 6th one year and runs to April 5th in the next year). The government takes away a certain percentage of what you earn (just under a third at the moment) after particular deductions are made. This means you don't pay tax on *all* your income, only what's left after the deductions or allowances are made. At the time of writing, you can get allowances for:

- yourself (you have to earn more than £2005 before you start paying income tax at all)
- your wife (it doesn't work for wives who want to claim for their husbands – see *Sexism* below)
- interest on mortgage repayments
- *some* expenses to do with your job.

The tax office will send you details when they send you a tax form to fill in.

Saving tax

The tax system is incredibly complicated and changes from year to year. The general rules for not paying more than you have to are:

■ make sure you're claiming all the allowances to which you're entitled

■ make sure you're claiming all the expenses you're allowed

■ tell the tax office (in the phone book under "INLAND REVENUE") if your circumstances change – for example a new job; a divorce; a marriage; a mortgage; self-employment and so on.

Some people get sent a tax return on which they have to give details for their income every year, others may only be sent one every few years so it's important to notify changes in your circumstances straight away.

A book like this can't give really detailed advice – look at tax guides which are updated every year and are available from newsagents and bookshops each Spring. Alternatively, get professional advice from an accountant (you'll have to pay but it's often worth it in terms of what you'll save unless your finances are very straightforward).

PAYE

If you work for an employer you'll probably be taxed under this system which stands for Pay As You Earn. It means your tax is deducted by your employer according to the tax code you're allocated by the Inland Revenue. When you first start a job you may be put on "emergency code" which means a lot more of your income is taken out than would be normally – but as soon as you get allocated a code it'll be adjusted so that you don't pay too much (you may even get a tax refund). Whenever you leave a job, make sure your employer gives you a P.45 – this is a form which explains your tax position to new employers or to the Department of Health and Social Security and Department of Employment if you have to claim benefits.

Self-employed

If you're working for yourself you still have to pay tax but you don't do it through PAYE. Each year you have to submit your accounts to the Inland Revenue, giving details of what you've earned and what your expenses were. It's almost certain that the expense of an accountant will be worthwhile if you're earning your living this way. What you should do anyway is to inform the tax office that you're self-employed, they'll send you a booklet explaining how to handle your tax affairs. Ask for *Starting in Business*.

Sexism

If you're married then only the husband will automatically be sent a tax form – the tax office normally treats husband and wife as one person after the tax year in which you marry. You and your partner can ask to have the wife's income taxed separately but unless you have a fairly high income between you it's not usually worth it. Getting married can either save you pounds on your tax bill or mean you pay more than you need to – look at specialist publications to find out what you can do to keep your tax low.

Help and advice

Saving and borrowing

Banks, building societies and Post Offices seem to compete with each other to see who can produce the most leaflets and booklets. The things produced by banks to try and attract young people's accounts can be quite useful in particular.

Consumer rights and debt problems

An increasing number of local councils are setting up *Consumer Advice Centres* in major shopping towns. Based in libraries, kiosks or shop-front premises, these can provide free, impartial advice and help on all your consumer problems – including ones not covered in this chapter like door to door sales, mail order catalogue buying and so on. They'll usually have useful leaflets too. Look in the phone book or ask at main libraries to see if one exists in your area, if not, contact your Citizens' Advice Bureau.

Much rarer are money advice centres which have trained workers who can give advice on handling debt problems – if your phone book doesn't have details, try the Citizens' Advice Bureau.

Your local council's *Trading Standards Officer* or *Consumer Protection Officer* can help in cases of misleading adverts or trade descriptions and trouble with short weight or measure. Details from the phone book. Their *Environmental Health Officer* is the person to see about bad food being sold or poor hygiene in shops or restaurants.

The *Consumers Association* is best known as publishers of *Which* magazine (see *Buying* above). They publish comparative surveys of all sorts of goods and services – worth checking in the library, and also a yearly tax guide. Membership costs £31. Write to 14 Buckingham Street, London WC2N 6DS. Tel: 01 839 1222.

The *National Consumer Council*, 18 Queen Anne's Gate, London SW1. Tel: 01 222 9501. This organisation was set up by the government to speak up for the consumer to government and sellers of goods and services. Doesn't deal with individual complaints. Get details from the above address of councils in Northern Ireland, Wales and Scotland.

The *Office of Fair Trading*, Field House, Bream's Buildings, London EC4A 1PR. This is another organisation set up by the government to look after consumers' interests. Produces lots of useful publications including *Fair Deal: A Shopper's guide* (price 95p from bookshops, published by HMSO) plus free leaflets available from many libraries and advice centres.

Consumerfacts (price 95p plus 60p postage and packing, published by the Careers and Occupational Information Centre, Moorfoot, Sheffield S1 4PQ) is a very clear and simple guide.

Tax

Contact your local tax office (in the phonebook under "INLAND REVENUE") for all questions about tax – they're more helpful than you might think and also produce a range of free publications – ask for a list.

Tax Saving Guides are produced every year (usually appearing around March), also look at the *Money* pages of many newspapers.

6. Education and training

Learning after 16 ■ why study? ■ information you need ■ school ■ further education ■ higher education ■ adult education ■ training schemes ■ training at work ■ help and advice

Learning after 16

After about fifteen thousand hours of compulsory schooling, you may have felt it was time to get away from education at the age of sixteen. Learning doesn't stop when you leave school though and many people come back to education and training again: you may go to college to learn a skill for work, do an evening class for fun or take lessons to play a new sport.

Profile

"I really hated school. Some of the teachers were OK but the head made so many petty rules. I left as soon as I could and I suppose I was lucky 'cause I got a shop job. But I realised quickly that I didn't want to do that the rest of my life so this year I've come to college here to try and get qualifications for a decent job. I'm doing a Diploma in Business Studies – book-keeping and things."

(*Kim, 18, Student at a further education college*)

The important thing about learning after you're sixteen is that you have some control over what you do and how you do it. You can study part-time, full-time or combine it with periods of work. More and more courses can be studied flexibly, at *your* pace, either in college or at home – depending on what's convenient. In addition there are many new opportunities after sixteen, for example:

■ you can study part-time while looking for work and not lose your benefit.

- you can go to college, even if you didn't get good results at school.
- you can consider a Youth Training Scheme combining work experience and training in a job, if you've just left school.
- you can get paid while you train for a job through TOPS courses if you're over nineteen.
- you can study for a degree with the Open University if you're over twenty one.
- you can study at a special college for adults if you're over 25.
- you can take special courses to prepare you for a degree if you haven't got A-levels.

Why study?

You may have lots of reasons for wanting to get more education and training:
- to pick up new skills (or brush up on those you have)
- to gain specialist knowledge about something
- to get the qualifications necessary or helpful for the jobs you want
- to acquire particular experience
- to meet new people
- to prove to others that you're not stupid
- to keep yourself occupied, either mentally or physically.

Whatever your reasons, remember it's not always necessary to do a formal 'course' in order to get what you want. You may be able to teach yourself – maybe by practising, by reading books or with the help of friends or workmates. You may even be able to exchange skills with someone you know: they teach you how to program their computer, for example, in return for you teaching them to play your guitar.

Information you need

If you do decide on a course or training programme you'll need to know:
- what's running where and when
- what it will cost
- your chances of getting financial help

- how much time it will take up
- how and when to apply (it can be almost a year in advance sometimes)
- what qualification (if any) the course leads to
- whether or not you'll be able to cope
- whether or not it's the right thing for you.

You can find out most of these things by reading the rest of this chapter which will explain where to look and who to ask. The last two points however, are more personal and you may not be too sure how you feel. Don't worry – it's not unusual and there are even courses to help you make such decisions and prepare you for a return to study after a break! See the section *Help and advice* at the end of the chapter for details.

School

About two thirds of people leave school at sixteen and some never bother with education and training again. More and more though, people are thinking about staying on longer. In the past, the only people really encouraged to stay were those who wanted to do A-levels, more O-levels or Scottish Highers. Although some schools are still like that, things are changing – lots are becoming more welcoming and have far more to offer. As well as the traditional subjects, schools are starting to run more courses to help you prepare for work or train you in the sort of skills you'll need in jobs (as well as those which can help you get jobs).

Unless you're convinced that school has nothing to offer you, it's worth weighing up the pros and cons:

Some of the good things about school are:

- you'll probably know quite a few people and have some idea of what it's like and what to expect
- when it comes to the traditional subjects (like English, maths, French, physics and so on), schools have lots of expertise and experience in teaching
- it shouldn't cost you anything if you're under 18 (colleges may expect you to buy all your own books and equipment).

Some of the bad things about school are:

- you won't normally get any money for staying on (but if your parents are hard up, get them to ask about an Education Maintenance Award from the local authority)

■ you may not want to study all day, every day – but almost all school courses are full-time

■ your friends may be leaving and you may not like the atmosphere of school and want to go somewhere that gives you more independence and treats you more like an adult

Probably the best advice is that if you've enjoyed school up to now and feel it has something to offer, then stay. But if you've been unhappy there, you may do better with a fresh start somewhere else.

If you want to stay at school, let the teachers know your plans as soon as possible. They ought to be able to advise you about your best subjects – and even if you can't stay, they will be able to suggest other school or college courses as alternatives.

Not all schools have sixth forms so you may have to go somewhere new anyway. In some areas there are schools especially for the over sixteens called "Sixth Form Colleges" – but if you are looking for a real change from a school environment, try Further Education.

Adults in schools
Very slowly, schools in more and more areas are allowing adult students into their classes. This is a really exciting idea – older people often have lots to contribute and teachers will treat everyone more considerately if there are other adults in the room. If you're over school age but know that local schools are running the courses you'd like to do, contact the head teacher and ask if you can sit in. You'll probably have to pay but if it is what's convenient for you, it will probably be worth it.

Further education (FE)

At its simplest, this means any sort of education for people over sixteen which isn't in school, in universities or entirely at work. In practice however, people don't usually include non-exam classes for adults nor degree level courses when they talk about FE.

Most FE is run from Colleges of Further Education (sometimes called Technical Colleges or simply "Colleges"). There are colleges in almost every town, run by the Local Education Authority (LEA). Most offer a wide range of courses but some specialise – for example, Agricultural Colleges. Most students in FE are between sixteen and nineteen but there are more and more older people enrolling too. You may come to college full-time, part-time or because your employer sends you one day a week or in a block as part of your training or apprenticeship. Some people also go to college through the Youth Training Scheme or TOPS (see *Training schemes* below).

Subjects to study

The range of subjects you can study in FE is much wider than in schools. Most of the courses are "vocational" (that means they're designed to prepare you for particular jobs) but, with the exception of Scotland, colleges usually run O and A-levels as well.

The qualifications for which you can study are usually accepted by employers nationally, even though you may not have heard of them at school. Some of the most common are:

- *Business and Technician Education Council (B/TEC)*: Awards certificates and Diplomas at various levels in everything from banking and retailing to building and science.
- *City & Guilds of London Institute*: Studying for your "City and Guilds" is often a part of craft training in things like bricklaying, motor mechanics, hairdressing and many other occupations.
- *Royal Society of Arts and Commerce (RSA)*: Awards qualifications in subjects like English and maths as well as office skills.
- *Scottish Vocational Education Council (SCOTVEC)*: This is the Scottish equivalent of B/TEC (see above).

There are lots of other specialist bodies representing particular occupations which award qualifications too.

Finding out more

All colleges produce information about what's on offer – ask for their "Prospectus". Tell them the courses or subjects in which you're interested – there may be extra leaflets. If you're unsure about a course (or even if the information does seem clear) it's worth going along to talk to the people running it. They won't mind (though it's best to make an appointment first) and you should get a better idea of what things are like before you apply. See if you can talk to students already doing the course to find out what they think of it. If the people running the courses can't arrange anything, try the Student Union at the college.

Getting in

Once you've chosen a course you must first make sure you meet the entry requirements – some courses insist you have particular qualifications before you can do them. If you've been out of education for a few years it's always worth asking if there are different arrangements for older students particularly if you've got experience which seems relevant. If it looks like there's nothing you can do, go back to the college and ask for advice from the teaching staff.

Most FE courses begin in September and it's often very difficult to join a class once it's started. You can usually enrol for part-time classes one or two weeks before they start just by post or by going along – see the prospectus for details. You may have to apply much earlier for full-time courses though – particularly if you want to do a popular course. Again, the prospectus should have details of how and when to do so.

What it will cost

If you're under eighteen and live in the local education authority (LEA) where the college is, you won't usually have to pay anything for full-time FE. If you want to study outside your LEA (that's your county, borough, or region, plus inner London) you may have to pay – it varies between places depending on the course and college – so ask at the college you'd like to attend.

Once you're over eighteen you'll usually have to pay course fees. These are sometimes very high and full-time study can be hard since you'll probably have to pay in advance. If money is a problem, always ask the college about reduced fees or paying fees each term – lots of places have special arrangements for unemployed people for example.

If you have a paid job and want to study part-time it's always worth asking your employer to help with the fees – particularly if you want to learn something that could be helpful in your work. Large employers will often agree to this and a few will even give you time off as well!

Profile

"I work in a Ministry of Agriculture office and they're really good. I get Friday afternoons off to come to college. I'm doing an O-level in sociology and they've paid all the costs."

(Lisa, 17, Clerical assistant)

As well as your course fees there may be other costs – exam entry fees, travel costs, equipment, tools or protective clothing, pens, paper and so on. Unlike schools, it's common to have to buy your own textbooks in FE – so try and get them second-hand if you can.

Financial help

With a few exceptions, there is no certainty that you'll get any money at all from your LEA to help you do an FE course – especially if you want to do a part-time course. Grants for FE are made at the *discretion* of the LEA where you live. (That means they *can* give you money but they don't *have* to!) Some areas are much more generous than others about who can get a grant, but these days when cash is tight, more and more places are turning people down.

You may be able to go to college through a government scheme which will pay the costs and give you some money to live on too. The Youth Training Scheme (for young people) and TOPS (for adults) are described later on.

Studying while unemployed

It is possible to study while you're unemployed without losing your supplementary or unemployment benefit. This can be a very complicated area: always double check that things haven't changed by asking your Citizens' Advice Bureau, Education Guidance Service (see *Help and advice* below) or the college concerned. Ask them about the "21-hour rule".

The law says that, in all but a very few special cases, you can't claim supplementary or unemployment benefit unless you're "available for work". (There may not be any jobs for which to be available, but that's the rule!) What this means is, you can't do an FE course full-time and still claim money.

You *can* study part-time when you're unemployed however, because of a regulation called the "21-hour rule". This means that you can go to college for up to twenty one hours of teaching per week without losing benefit *if* you could take up a job immediately if one came up.

To take advantage of the rule you have to have been unemployed and receiving supplementary benefit for three months before doing the course. During that time you may study part-time for up to twelve hours a week – but only if it's on a *different* course to the one you want to do under the "21-hour rule"! The one exception to this qualifying period is for people leaving a YTS scheme who may move straight away onto a "21-hour rule" course.

Confused? So are a lot of people. If you're worried about signing up for too much part-time study, get help from the college (though there are rumours that some colleges are making up their own rules about who they'll count as part-timers).

Higher education (HE)

This describes courses which lead to a degree (such as Bachelor of Arts – BA, or Bachelor of Science – BSc.) plus some diplomas and professional qualifications which are equivalent to degrees. The majority of courses take three years of full-time study but there are an increasing number of part-time courses over longer periods.

HE courses are run in universities, polytechnics and colleges or institutes of higher education. Unlike further education, it's very common for people, particularly school leavers, to go to a higher education centre away from the area where they normally live.

Although some HE courses (like medicine or engineering) may train people for specific jobs it's not unusual for people to do a course in one subject and find a job in something different. This is because a degree is often a general level of entry to many jobs – no matter what the subject.

Applying for a degree

This can be a complicated and long-winded business. The first point is that you have to apply as much as a year in advance. Most courses begin in September and you should apply for university courses between then and December in the year *before* you want to start. You can carry on applying for courses outside universities after that date – but the popular ones fill up quickly.

Exactly how you should apply depends on which sort of place you want to do your degree and what you want to study.

■ For university courses you just have to fill in one form and can apply to as many as 5 places. Get the details and form from the Universities Central Council on Admissions (address at end of chapter). The exceptions to this are if you want to go to the University of Buckingham (apply direct), to Strathclyde, Glasgow or Aberdeen (see their prospectuses – in some cases you apply direct) or the Open University.

■ For the Open University, apply direct. OU degree courses start in February and you should apply as soon as possible before October in the year before you want to start. The OU address is at the end of the chapter.

■ For polytechnic courses check the prospectuses. A new centralised system will be starting this year for entry to courses in 1986. This should mean you won't have to make lots of separate applications.

■ For courses at Colleges and Institutes of Higher Education apply directly. You can apply to as many places as you like.

Central application schemes also exist in England and Wales for courses outside universities in the following subjects:

■ teacher training (apply through the Central Register and Clearing House).

■ social work (apply through the Central Council for Education and training in Social Work).

■ BA courses in Art and Design (apply through the Art and Design Registry).

The prospectuses of the places running these courses have full details of how to apply.

Approach these application forms just like you would ones for jobs – with care. They can be complicated so it's important to get it right.

Finding out more

These are two books you can use to find out which courses are running where. These are:

■ the *Directory of First Degree Courses*, published by the Central Council for National Academic Awards (CNAA) (address at end of chapter), which lists most degree courses at polytechnics and colleges or institutes of HE.

■ The *UCCA Handbook*, published by the Universities Central Council on Admissions, (address at end of chapter), which lists almost all university first degrees.

Both these books are free. Unfortunately, the system has a few loose ends and a very few courses won't be listed in either book – which is why you'll find it helpful to talk to teachers or careers officers if you can.

Once you've tracked down places which run the course you want, you can write to them for their prospectus which will give you full details. If the only place which seems to do the course you want is miles away and you don't want to move, or if it's only running full-time and you want to study part-time, don't forget the Open University. OU courses are part-time and can be done in your home wherever you live. The OU is unique in other ways too, described in more detail below.

Who can do a degree?
HE is a competitive part of the system. Every year more people apply than there are places. Admission is very much geared up to school leavers with O and A-levels or Scottish Highers – but if that doesn't include you, don't give up:

■ a growing number of FE colleges are starting to run specially designed preparatory courses accepted by some institutions as alternatives to A-levels. With names like "Access courses" or "Gateway courses", some are specially designed for people from ethnic minorities. These are all listed in a book called *Second Chances for Adults* (see the section on *Help and advice* for details).

■ if you're over twenty one, you can enrol on an Open University degree course without needing to have any qualifications – they take people on a first come first served basis.

■ if you're over twenty five, the regulations about needing school leaver's qualifications don't apply but you will need to show evidence of recent study that's relevant. This *could* be part-time A-levels but might instead be at a special residential college for adults (the section on *Adult education* has more details).

Be sure you understand the instructions before you do anything. Some of the books listed at the end of the chapter say a lot about how to apply so look at them too. They will also tell you how to handle any interviews you may get.

Financial help
If you've not done a degree before and are normally resident in Britain then HE won't cost you anything if you're on a full-time course. The cost of the course is paid and you get a grant to live on from your LEA (in Scotland, the Scottish Education Department and in Northern Ireland, the Education and Library Boards). Write to them for the forms when you apply for your course.

You can try for financial help towards part-time courses but don't expect too much success. Open University students will probably

get help toward the cost of their summer schools. If you're
working, it's always worth asking your employer for help.

Adult education

Part-time classes for adults are run during the day as well as in the
evening and cover a vast range of subjects. Some are run by the
education authority, some by an organisation called the Workers
Educational Association, some by universities and many more
besides. Groups and classes meet in schools, village halls, colleges
and, in some areas, special adult centres. You can learn practical
skills, languages, sports, about literature, women's studies or
history – and if what you want isn't available, organisers are often
prepared to set up a course if you can show them there's the demand.
Some courses lead to examinations (especially O and A-levels) but
not all of them.

To find out what's running near you, contact the Education
Department at your county or borough council. Ask for "Adult
Education" or "Community Education" (the title varies). Local
libraries are another good place – they should have details of *all*
organisations running courses.

Anyone who's left school can do adult education (if you haven't
and want to start, get your head teacher's permission). It will cost
you money – exactly what varies from place to place, but if you're
under eighteen or not working, there are probably reductions – so
ask.

There's another sort of adult education too – special residential
colleges for people over twenty five which run one or two year
courses in subjects like sociology, economics, literature and
philosophy. You don't have to have A-levels or Scottish Highers to
get in and if you're accepted, you are entitled to a grant.

Full details of these courses and colleges are given in *Second
Chances for Adults* (see *Help and advice* below).

Training schemes

If you want training to help you get a job or change your job there
are two schemes run by the Manpower Services Commission
which could help. YTS (the Youth Training Scheme) is for young
people and TOPS (Training Opportunities Scheme) is for people

over nineteen. Neither costs anything and you get a training allowance.

Who are they for?

YTS is run throughout Britain (there's a similar scheme in Northern Ireland) and is open to any sixteen year old school leaver who wants to join, some seventeen year-olds and disabled school or college leavers up to the age of twenty one.

TOPS courses are also run throughout Britain with a similar scheme in Northern Ireland. They're open to anyone over the age of nineteen who's been out of full-time education for at least 2 years. You have to take tests to get on the courses and waiting lists are often long. If you're worried about your reading, spelling or maths, ask about preparatory courses to help you. You don't have to be unemployed to do TOPS but since most courses are full-time you'd have to be prepared to give up your job.

What do they offer?

YTS is a two-year programme offering a mixture of training and planned work experience. Courses are offered by all sorts of employers, by colleges and by voluntary organisations. Although you get at least sixty five days "off the job" training in a college, skillcentre or somewhere else, the majority of the training is done "on the job" as part of the work experience. This is one reason why YTS comes in for criticism – lots of people think that they're not getting properly trained and are simply used as cheap labour. In some cases this will be true – it's certainly the case that the employers are not monitored closely enough, in other cases it may not be correct – you'll have to decide for yourself.

TOPS courses vary in length but the longest last a year. They're run in colleges of further education and in the Manpower Services Commission's own "Skillcentres". It's likely that changes to TOPS will be made soon but at present, the range of courses is enormous; engineering, office skills, electrical, hotel and catering, management, computing and so on. There are also special courses for disabled people, for women and for people wanting to start their own businesses. In addition if there's no TOPS course available they are sometimes prepared to sponsor you to do an ordinary college course under their "Infill" scheme. What all the courses have in common though is that they're intended to improve your job prospects – helping you update or extend the skills you have or teach you new ones. If what you want isn't available locally you may be able to live away from home to do your course.

What do you get paid?

At the time of writing, the minimum training allowance for people on YTS is £26.25 but it looks like this figure may rise shortly. All the same it's easy to see why people say that YTS trainees are exploited – after all, the value of the work they do is usually far greater than this and the trainee doesn't cost the employer anything. In some areas and workplaces, local trade unions or councils have persuaded the people running schemes to "top up" the allowance to a more acceptable level. In addition, trainees on YTS can claim back any money above £3 that they spend on travel each week and if you're on the scheme you're entitled to paid holidays.

TOPS training allowances vary according to your circumstances – you get extra for your dependents for example. At present the basic allowance is £38.00 and you can get an extra £24.70 if you have an "adult dependent" who's not working or on a low wage. Full details are given in leaflet TD L91 available from Jobcentres and Employment Offices. The MSC has also started to introduce some part-time TOPS courses aimed at people out of work. They don't cost you anything – but you don't get paid, you just stay on the dole.

Where does it lead?

Unless more work is created, the depressing fact is that for some people, training is going to lead nowhere. We may soon have one of the best trained dole queues in the world. However, it's important not to get too depressed – TOPS courses have a good record in helping people find work – after all, they only run courses in things where you're likely to get a job at the end of it. YTS is more difficult – some people are employees when they start and do YTS as part of their apprenticeship, others get taken on at the places they've worked when the training ends – but in many areas jobs simply don't exist in sufficient numbers and YTS doesn't help much. On balance, YTS is probably worth a try – you can always leave if you find the place isn't training you (you can do this twice if necessary and go onto another scheme) but if it's a good scheme – and plenty are, the skills you learn will improve your chances. Even if a YTS Certificate can't guarantee you a job it won't do any harm and going on a scheme may allow you to learn and make contacts which boost your prospects. At present you don't have to do YTS, although if you turn down too many offers of places you could risk losing your supplementary benefit for six weeks (if this happens, get help immediately from the Citizens' Advice Bureau). In the end you have to decide what your options are and the advantages and disadvantages of each.

Finding out more
Your Careers Service can tell you more about YTS and the schemes available in your area — also keep an eye on the local paper since some schemes advertise directly.

Details of the wide range of opportunities available through TOPS are available from Jobcentres and Employment Offices. They also handle applications. Ask to see a Training Adviser or, if you're disabled, a Disablement Resettlement Officer.

Training at work

Lots of jobs require the people who do them to be trained. Sometimes this will simply mean someone showing you what to do as you go along, in other cases the employer will have special rooms or workshops set aside for training. Large shops often open late one day a week – the first hour being used for staff training.

Apprenticeships
When you go into some jobs, you'll be employed under a special sort of contract – an apprenticeship. For many years, these have been the way for school leavers to start and learn a skilled trade (printing or carpentry for instance) and if you're more than seventeen you may find it virtually impossible to get one. Because of unemployment, apprenticeships are hard to get anyway – if you've left school already it may be too late.

An apprenticeship is an agreement between you, your parents or guardians and an employer. You agree to stay with the employer for a set period (often 3 years, sometimes more) and the employer agrees to put you through a recognized course of training which often includes one day a week at an FE College (see above) to study for exams. You also get paid a nationally accepted wage – though not as much as skilled workers.

Since many apprenticeships are in jobs which in the past were usually done by men, you may find problems if you're a woman. Look at Chapter 7 (*Rights and laws*) for what to do if you believe there's been sex discrimination. In addition, an organisation called Women in Manual Trades may be able to offer advice as well as support. Contact them at 52/54 Featherstone Street, London EC1. Tel: 01 251 9192.

The whole apprenticeship scene is changing at the moment – use the Careers Service for up to date advice and information.

Open Tech

This isn't an organisation or a training scheme – it's a new way of providing workers with part-time training at their own pace. Open Tech is a series of projects developed by industry and education to train people through "distance learning". Like Open University courses, this means that you do most of your study on your own, with the help of books, workpacks, videos and so on. You may also be able to arrange to go into a nearby college at times convenient to you for help.

Since Open Tech is so new, nobody knows how well it's going to work yet. If this form of training would be convenient for you, ask your employer if something could be arranged or write to the Open Tech Unit, Room W601 Manpower Services Commission, Moorfoot, Sheffield S1 4PQ. Already there are packages available for everyone from innkeepers and library assistants to people working in tourism and printing.

Help and advice

Places

If you're already in education, make use of your teachers or lecturers as well as trying:

■ *the Careers Service.* Look in the phonebook under "CAREERS". Tell them you're interested in further or higher education – there may be a different person to see.

■ *Educational Guidance Services* are organisations which exist in some areas to provide free, impartial advice and help about educational opportunities – particularly for people with few qualifications. They don't exist everywhere so look out for publicity or look at the list in the book *Second Chances for Adults* (below).

- *your Local Education Authority* (for information about grants, adult education etc.). Look in the phonebook under your county, borough or regional council's education department. There's a different organisation for people living in central London boroughs – the Inner London Education Authority.
- *the Jobcentre or Employment Office* for information about TOPS. Look in the phone book under "MANPOWER SERVICES COMMISSION".
- *the National Union of Students*, 461 Holloway Road, London N7 6LJ. Tel: 01 272 8900.

Books

For an introduction to just about every form of education and training after school, look at *Second Chances for Adults 1984/85* (£9.95, published by the National Extension College). Libraries will have a copy.

For information about Higher Education courses and places, look at *The Student Book 1985/86* (£6.95, published by Macmillan).

For information on applying to a university, together with forms, send for *How to apply for admission to a university*, free from UCCA, PO Box 28, Cheltenham, Glos. GL50 1HY.

For information and an application form for Open University degrees, send for *Guide for applicants for BA degree courses*, free from the Open University Admissions Office, PO Box 49, Milton Keynes MK7 6AD.

For details of almost all degree courses outside universities, send for *Directory of first degree courses* and also *Opportunities in Higher Education for Mature Students*, free from the Publications Officer, CNAA, 344/345 Grays Inn Road, London WC1X 8BP.

For information and advice aimed particularly at women wishing to return to education, look at *It's never too late, a practical guide to continuing education for women of all ages*, by Joan Perkin (£3.95, published by Impact Books).

7. Rights and laws

The law ■ the police ■ coming of age ■ racism
and discrimination ■ sexism and discrimination
■ help and advice

The law

There are laws concerning just about every activity you can think of
and it's not possible to say much in just a few pages. In addition, the
legal systems in Scotland and in Northern Ireland are different from
that of England and Wales and aren't covered in the chapter at all.

One important thing to get clear is that there are basically two
sorts of law: criminal law and civil law. Breaches of criminal law
(crimes) are seen as offences against society as a whole. Police are
employed to prevent them and criminal courts punish people who
are found to have broken them. These sorts of offences include
theft, fraud, murder and so on.

Breaches of civil law (called "torts") aren't "crimes" – but, you
could say, a more private affair. They are actions brought by one or
more people against other individuals or groups for things like:
nuisance, trespass, negligence, libel, breach of contract.

The police don't deal with these offences (that's why if your
neighbours have a wild party the police often can't do more than ask
them to turn the noise down) and there's a different set of courts.
These don't punish people – they award damages (money) to those
who've been wronged, to be paid by the offenders.

Ignorance of the law isn't accepted as an excuse for breaking it –
but even though most people don't know much about the law, they
don't seem to break it very often. It's in your interest to find out
about the law – firstly so that you can keep out of trouble and
secondly so that you can use it to protect yourself. Unfortunately,
being aware of your rights and of what society expects isn't easy –
lawyers spend much of their time trying to work out *exactly* what
particular laws mean and it's hard enough for the rest of us to even
understand what they're saying!

The police

It's the job of the police to prevent crime and to try and catch people who commit crime. This isn't an easy job and sometimes, in trying to do it, they make mistakes. In order to do their job better the police sometimes say they need more power – but giving them more power means that the rest of us have less freedom.

Most of your contact with the police is likely to be without any problems. You may want:

■ to report your bike has been stolen
■ to give them information about something you've seen
■ to ask them to suggest ways of protecting your home.

There may be occasions though when the police take an interest in you even when you've not done anything wrong. Statistically, this is more likely to be the case if you're:

■ male　　　　　　■ working class　　■ living in a city.
■ under twenty five　■ black

When this happens you need to know your rights.

Near the end of 1984, a law called the Police and Criminal Evidence Act was passed in England and Wales which gave the police more powers but it's too early to know yet how these are being used in practice. Because of this, the information below is a little general.

On the street

The police can stop and search you if they think you've got:

■ drugs　　　　　　　■ stolen goods
■ offensive weapons　　■ burglary tools

in your possession. They must tell you why – so ask. If you think they're doing it simply to hassle you, get advice as soon as you can. If you've not done anything wrong, publicise what's happened – tell teachers and lecturers, youth and community workers, religious leaders, councillors, journalists or anyone else with influence in your neighbourhood who can raise a fuss.

If the police start questioning you on the street, don't tell them anything other than your name and address (in some circumstances you have to do this so it's best to do so anyway). Don't get upset and start shouting, even if you feel embarrassed or provoked. Stay polite, ask them why they want to know and when you think things have gone far enough, don't answer.

In the home

The police have no right to enter your home unless you've invited them in unless they:

- ■ have a warrant from a magistrate (ask to see it)
- ■ believe someone's in there who they can arrest without a warrant (that's someone suspected of a serious crime)
- ■ want to stop or prevent serious violence or breach of the peace.

Going to the station

The only way you can be made to go to a police station against your will in England and Wales is if you've been arrested – and if they arrest you, they have to tell you why. If they simply want to ask you questions, you don't have to go. Unless you're certain you've done nothing wrong, go quietly if you've been arrested. If you try to resist or run off it'll make things harder for you.

In the station

At the station you'll probably be questioned but if you're under seventeen this should only be done in the presence of a parent, solicitor, youth or social worker or adult friend so refuse to say anything until then.

The new law gives the police the right to search you for drugs or weapons and take fingerprints, photos or body samples without your consent. They can also hold you for up to twenty four hours without charging you with any offence (longer for serious offences if a court approves). For minor offences you'll almost always be allowed to phone your family or friends but for serious offences the police may deny people access to you for up to thirty six hours. When you can call someone, ask them to arrange to get you a solicitor and until she or he arrives don't say or sign anything – it's your right to remain silent. Most importantly of all, NEVER confess to something you didn't do just to get away from the station – you'll find it very difficult to change your mind later. (See *Help and advice* for information about getting legal help.)

If you're charged

Ask your solicitor to apply for bail. This means they let you out if you or someone else (parents or friends) promises to pay money if you don't turn up at court when they say. Unless you're homeless or have been in trouble before or can't find anyone who'll guarantee the money, you'll probably get bail.

At the court

Unless you're under seventeen, your case will start off being heard in a Magistrates' Court. All small offences are tried in this court although you do have the option to go to a higher court (the Crown Court) and be tried by a jury. Very serious offences, such as murder, will get sent to the Crown Court automatically. There are no juries in Magistrates' Courts – instead your case is heard by Justices of the Peace (JPs). Most JPs are ordinary local people who do the job part–time and won't usually have any legal qualifications at all. They have been trained though, and are advised by a court clerk who is a professional lawyer. In some large towns there are also full-time magistrates who are legally qualified.

Unless the charge is very trivial you should always get a lawyer to represent you (see *Help and advice* below).

Profile

"I was out on the street and had stopped to watch a demonstration go by. It was all pretty peaceful but then the police started to try and move on some people who had stopped marching. They started grabbing people and then things got a bit out of hand because people were trying to get away. I got caught up and was trying to move away fast when I got nicked. I kept on saying that I was only watching and that it was a mistake but they didn't listen. I got taken off to the police station and was kept there for a couple of hours and then they simply let me go. I was so relieved to get out I wasn't even angry at the time".

(Adam, 21, Student)

Coming of age

As you get older you start to get more rights and responsibilities.

By the time you are fifteen

You can:
- have your own bank account
- be convicted of a crime

- enter a pub (but not buy alcohol)
- work part-time
- own an air rifle
- pawn things in a pawn shop

but the changes really start with your next birthday.

When you're sixteen

You can:

- leave school
- get a full-time job (but not work nights)
- join a trade union
- claim supplementary benefit
- leave home with your parents' permission (or without, in Scotland)
- buy cigarettes and tobacco
- drink beer, wine or cider with a meal in a pub or restaurant (eighteen in Northern Ireland)
- get married with your parents' permission
- consent to sexual intercourse (girls)
- choose your own doctor
- buy fireworks
- decide for yourself whether to have an abortion
- sell scrap metal
- collect donations for charity
- drive a moped or tractor
- take part in public performances without a licence
- hold your own premium bonds
- choose your own religion
- join the armed forces (boys) with your parents' consent.

When you're seventeen

You can:

- be sent to prison
- go into a betting shop (but not bet)
- drive a car or motorbike
- apply for a private pilot's licence
- be a street trader (not in all areas)
- join the armed forces (girls) with parents' consent
- buy or hire firearms or ammunition (with a licence).

When you're eighteen

You can:

- leave home
- get married
- vote in local and national elections
- join the armed forces
- sit on a jury
- be tattooed

- make a will
- buy alcoholic drinks
- get a mortgage
- give blood
- bet or work in a betting shop
- emigrate
- change your name
- go to "18" films

- hold a credit card and take out HP agreements without a guarantor.

When you're twenty one

You can:

- stand as a candidate for the local council or parliament
- adopt a child
- drive a bus or lorry
- consent to homosexual activity in private with another male (except in Northern Ireland)
- hold a licence to sell alcohol
- be sentenced to life imprisonment for serious offences.

Racism and discrimination

When things are organised in such a way that some people are denied fair treatment because of their race or colour, it's a sign of racism. Too many people face intolerance and injustice because of this. Although the law is meant to stop the worst aspects of racial discrimination, there are people in positions of power whose prejudice means that racial inequality is still with us, even though Britain is a multi-racial society.

So long as people's prejudices go unchallenged the problems will remain. This means that while the law is important, it's not enough to sit back and wait for it to work. Lots of the things you may have heard about race relations are quite simply myths and one very simple thing you can do is to find out the facts. Write for a list of free publications from the Commission for Racial Equality (address in *Help and advice*). For some ideas about ways of combatting racism, send for *What can I do to challenge Racism* (free) from the Anti-Racist

Programme, Greater London Council, County Hall, London SE1 7PB. Also ask the Community Relations Council if there's one in your area (look in your phone book).

What the law says

In 1976 a law called the Race Relations Act was passed in England, Scotland and Wales to try and protect people from racial discrimination as:

■ job applicants
■ house buyers
■ employees
■ tenants or would–be tenants
■ members or would–be members of clubs or trade unions
■ students or trainees
■ customers or clients of anyone providing goods, services or facilities.

The act doesn't necessarily cover *religious* differences (even when linked closely to race).

The law says that there are various kinds of discrimination which aren't allowed:

■ *direct discrimination*: This means treating some people less favourably than others on the grounds of their race.
■ *indirect discrimination*: This means having rules and regulations which affect one racial group in a substantially worse way than another (even if it's not intentional) and which can't be justified on non–racial grounds.
■ *discrimination by victimisation*: This means treating people badly because they've complained about discrimination or been witnesses in cases of discrimination (or if they intend to do these things).

Racial harassment

In some areas people live in fear of abuse, and attacks on both themselves, their families and their property simply because of their race. If this is true for you or your friends it's sometimes not easy to know what to do:

■ most small incidents or threats may never get reported to anyone since you may feel it's impossible to do much.
■ even when serious incidents are reported you may feel that the police don't respond quickly enough to help or give your complaint the attention it deserves.

Racial harassment isn't something to be endured (although you may be scared that combatting it may make things worse for you). If you're not able to do anything on your own, try to join with others in your neighbourhood to isolate the racists and defend yourselves. Monitor the extent of the problem and try to get the help and support of local councillors, youth and community workers and journalists in your campaign.

There is a law which makes "incitement to racial hatred" an offence but it can only be used by the government or with their consent – so it's not very common. If you can identify the source of problems (such as racist newsheets), campaign against the people who publish them and for the law to be used.

What to do about racial discrimination
If you've experienced discrimination you don't have to put up with it – complain. It may well be a bit of a battle to prove your case but the effort is worth it – one of the ways to change things is to let people know that they can't get away with discrimination.

If your case is to do with employment, take it up with an Industrial Tribunal within three months of it happening. Get form IT.1 from your local Jobcentre or Employment Office to do this. If the complaint is about something other than employment, you have to go to court.

In order to improve your chances of success, you'll find it helpful to get expert advice. Try:
- the Citizens' Advice Bureau
- your trade union (for cases to do with employment and sometimes others)
- a solicitor (see *Legal help* below)
- the Commission for Racial Equality (see *Help and advice* for details but if you've got a local Community Relations Council, try here first)
- self-help groups, law centres and community workers where these exist.

Sexism and discrimination

Some people believe that you should act in certain ways, like and dislike certain things simply because you're a woman or because you're a man. This is sexism – it's the idea that simply because of your biology you're particularly suited to some things and not to others and that you're likely to have particular attitudes. In reality, of course, when they're given the same opportunities and encouragement, both women and men can do most things equally well. The problem, however, is that women have always tended to have fewer chances and face more restrictions than men.

There's a long way to go before real equality between the sexes is reached but two laws have started to move things in the right direction. These are the 1975 Sex Discrimination Act and the 1984 Equal Pay Act (which added to an earlier equal pay law of 1969).

What the law says
The new Equal Pay Act tries to end discrimination in the areas of pay and work conditions like hours, sick leave and holidays. It applies to almost everyone at work – you don't have to have been working for a set period before you're covered. The law says that you should get the same pay and conditions as people of the opposite sex working for your employer if:
■ your work is the same or broadly similar
■ your job has been rated the same under a job evaluation study
■ your work is of equal value (in terms of effort, skill or decision making required).
The second law – the Sex Discrimination Act, makes sex discrimination in Great Britain illegal in areas like:
■ employment
■ education and training
■ buying a home
■ buying from shops
■ claiming social security.
It outlaws:
■ *direct discrimination:* This is when a woman is treated less favourably than a man simply because of her sex.
■ *indirect discrimination*: This is treatment which may seem to be equal but which in practice discriminates considerably against one or other sex.
One important exception to the law in the field of employment is that it doesn't apply to small employers with not more than five people (including part-timers) working there.

What to do about sex discrimination
If you feel that you deserve equal pay with someone else in your workplace, try taking the matter up through your trade union first or see your employer. If you're not satisfied with explanations that

the jobs compared are different, you can take the case to an Industrial Tribunal (get form IT.1 from your Jobcentre or Employment Office anytime up to six months after you leave the job). It's illegal for your employer to victimise you for doing this. If your claim is successful you'll be awarded equal pay or equal treatment.

You may want to get help from your union, the Citizens' Advice Bureau or a lawyer in pressing your case.

If you want to complain under the Sex Discrimination Act you have to take your case to court unless it's to do with employment (in which case you go to an Industrial Tribunal in the same way as for equal pay, described above). You have to make your complaint within six months of the discrimination happening and if you're successful, you could get compensation or the organisation which discriminated against you may be made to treat everyone equally.

Get help and advice about fighting your case from your union, the Citizens' Advice Bureau and from the Equal Opportunities Commission (see *Help and advice* for more details).

Sexual harassment

Too often this issue isn't treated seriously enough and you may find it hard going to get things done to prevent harrassment. The topic is important however, because if women are seen simply as passive sex objects, then real equality is impossible.

If you're subject to sexual harassment at work, don't accept it as part of the job – bring up the issue within your trade union. More and more unions are beginning to recognise the extent of this problem and are prepared to help. If the union has got a policy about this, make sure that it's stuck to and if there's no policy, try to get one passed. If it's your colleagues who're the problem, make contact with other women workers in your workplace, your industry or your locality to find out ways of overcoming the problems. More and more cities and large towns have Women's Centres where you can make contact and there's also a growing number of groups for women working in particular occupations. These are often found in jobs where women workers are in the minority. For up to date information about these, contact the Voluntary Organisations Unit at the Equal Opportunities Commission (address in *Help and advice*).

Help and advice

It's difficult to recommend many books to look at because there's always a danger that they'll be out of date because of changes to the law. This means that it's hard to help yourself and you're probably best off getting advice. Nevertheless, you'll be able to find out more from:

Know your rights published by the *National Council for Civil Liberties*, 95p. This is a handy-sized plastic wallet with thirteen factsheets outlining your rights on many basic issues. Include 20p for post and packing when you send for it from NCCL, 21 Tabard Street, London SE1 4LA. Tel: 01 403 3888. Ask also for details of other publications including:

■ *Your Rights at Work* (£1.95)
■ *Race Relations Rights* (£1.95)
■ *First Rights – a Guide to Legal Rights for Young People* (£1.50).

In Scotland, get details of publications from the Scottish Council for Civil Liberties, 146 Holland Street, Glasgow G2 4NG. Tel: 041 332 5960.

A thicker reference book is *The Penguin Guide to the Law* by John Pritchard, published by Penguin Books, £6.95. You'll probably want to borrow this from the library rather than buy it.

Local help

For routine enquiries you can't beat your local Citizens' Advice Bureau for accurate, independent and free help on all aspects of the law and your rights. If they can't help, they'll be able to put you in touch with someone who can. For professional legal help try:

■ *Law centres*: Run by solicitors, these centres provide free legal help especially in subjects like housing disputes, employment problems and difficulties with benefits. They are usually less formal than other professional help but the problem is that most are located in big cities and there may not be one near you (ask the Citizens' Advice Bureau or your library). Even though they do an excellent job it's unlikely that any new centres will be set up – and those that do exist may be threatened by government spending cuts.

■ *Solicitors*: There are solicitors in just about every town in England and Wales (look under "s" in the yellow pages). The problem is that many people feel a bit scared about contacting solicitors and worry about the cost. Because of this there are a couple of schemes to try and make things easier.

If you've not been charged with any offence and just want legal advice, you can see a solicitor at low cost (or no cost) under the *Green Card Scheme*. You can use this for help if you want to prepare a case for a tribunal, if someone sues you or if you want to see if you can use the law against someone else. Check that the solicitor you approach operates this scheme when you fix up the appointment.

If you've been charged with a criminal offence you should always get professional assistance. If you're on a low income you should be able to get *legal aid* to pay for a lawyer to prepare your case and represent you in court. The amount (if anything) you pay depends on your income and commitments. Help isn't automatic though.

You can get the forms to apply for help from courts or from most solicitors anytime after you've been charged until your case is heard.

National organisations

For information about the law and sex discrimination plus ways of fighting prejudice (including practical help in some cases), contact the *Equal Opportunities Commission*. This organisation was set up by the government and publishes many free and priced leaflets and reports (send for a list) plus a free magazine *Equality Now*. Contact the EOC, Overseas House, Quay Street, Manchester M3 3HN. Tel: 061 833 9244.

There's a separate EOC for Northern Ireland, write to Lindsay House, Callender Street, Belfast BT1 5DT. Tel: (0232) 42752.

For information about the law and racial discrimination plus ways of fighting racism, contact the *Commission for Racial Equality*. This organisation was set up by the government and works to make sure the law is upheld. It produces many free and priced publications (ask for a list) and can sometimes offer practical help. The main office of the Commission is at Elliot House, 10–12 Allington Street, London SW1E 5EH. Tel: 01 828 7022. Many areas of Britain also have Community Relations Councils which provide information and support. Ask at a library, Citizens' Advice Bureau or look in the phone book. The CRE will also put you in touch.

A self-help group for young people is the *National Association of*

Young People in Care. For details of activities and ways of getting involved, contact NAYPIC London Office, Children's Legal Centre, 20 Compton Terrace, London N1 2UN. Tel: 01 359 6251. (The Children's Legal Centre itself will provide advice on how laws in many fields affect young people.)

8. Having a say

Why bother with politics? ■ where decisions are made ■ how to influence the decision makers ■ political parties ■ pressure groups ■ community action ■ making contact

Why bother with politics?

Just about every day, someone somewhere is making decisions which will affect your life. Sometimes the people making the choices won't be accountable to anyone, but in plenty of cases they've been put into positions of power by people like you. Sometimes the decisions they make won't matter to you at all, at other times they could change your whole life.

Some people think that politics is only about parliament and town halls – they're wrong. Politics is about power:

■ who has it (and why)
■ who wants it (and why)
■ how the people who have power use it
■ how the people without power can try to get it.

Getting involved in politics then means having a say about all the things which affect your life. This will certainly involve government but it's far wider than that, covering all the people or organisations which have authority over you – which may include schools or colleges, workplaces and maybe even the family.

If you don't mind other people running your life for you then you can afford to ignore politics. You shouldn't moan then about:

■ what level of taxes you pay
■ what kind of education you or your children get
■ the prices you pay in shops
■ the jobs you can't find
■ the pollution of air, land and water
■ how well the streets are cleaned
■ how long you have to wait for a hospital operation
■ any discrimination you face

■ the power station/road/American air base/peace camp/sewage plant that's planned near your home.

Many decisions are made *in your name* – so it seems sensible to make your voice heard to support or challenge them. Even when you can't have any control over the decision, you may still have some influence by making sure people know how it will affect you or others.

Where decisions are made

In a society like ours it's sometimes difficult to see how particular decisions are arrived at. Sometimes what happens in theory is rather different from what happens in practice – and anyway, it's changing all the time.

Some of the decisions which affect us aren't even made in this country! The UK is part of two very important alliances of countries:

■ NATO, a military alliance
■ the EEC (or Common Market), an economic alliance.

In addition, there are other international forces (foreign governments, international companies for example) which can put pressure on our government.

In theory however, any decision can be overruled or ignored by parliament (the House of Commons and House of Lords). Only parliament can make laws that affect the whole country – even when there are local bye-laws, they only exist because parliament allows them. It also decides on taxes – how much they should be and on what things (income, beer, company profits and so on). The government then uses the money raised to do its work. Parliament decides the framework – but it doesn't actually run much.

Local government actually runs and pays for most of the services we use – things like roads, education, the fire service, cleaning streets and emptying dustbins, social services, swimming pools and parks and housing. There are different levels of local government – ranging from county and regional councils to parish councils. Some parts of local government are likely to change in the next couple of years so it's not worth giving more details. In addition, local government works very differently in Northern Ireland. The money local government needs to run things comes from parliament in the form of a grant and through the rates (a sort of local tax on property) – although parliament controls how much can be raised.

There are a whole number of other organisations or bodies which can affect our lives and which everyone pays for through taxes – but which are sometimes forgotten when people talk about politics. These include:
- the National Health Service
- the police
- the Manpower Services Commission
- the court system and judges.

As well as "official" organisations and government all sorts of other people's decisions affect our lives and it's easy to feel that you don't have much say about things as a *consumer, worker, student, trainee* or *benefit claimant*.

But the following section looks at the ways you can take more control of your own life and that of your community.

How to influence the decision makers

There are really two sides to this:
- influencing people who are accountable to you
- influencing the rest.

Elections

Elections are what gives government, both local and national, the right to govern. All local councillors and members of the House of Commons have been elected by groups of people to act on their behalf. In addition, they have to be re-elected periodically if they want to continue – so standing in elections and voting are an obvious way of putting your views across to the government. (There's one bit of parliament which isn't elected however – the House of Lords. People in the Lords have inherited the right to sit in parliament or have been appointed for life – none of them are accountable to anybody.)

Every Member of Parliament (MP), Member of the European Parliament (MEP) and Councillor represents a particular area (called a constituency) and is elected by the people who live there.

Voting

You can vote in elections if you're:

■ a citizen of Britain or the Irish Republic
■ eighteen or over on the day of the election
■ included in the register of electors
■ not disqualified (if you're serving a long prison sentence for example).

At every election some people find they can't vote because they're not on the electoral register. This list of people allowed to vote is updated each year and runs from February to February. In the Autumn, a form is sent to every household for listing voters. Make sure your name gets included – even if you're only seventeen now. You can check your name's down as soon as the draft list is published in November. Ask for it in libraries, council offices and main post offices. If you're not included you can get them to put you in (if you're in time) before the final list comes out.

Students who live away from home during term time can be registered in both places.

Whenever there's an election you get sent a card telling you when and where to vote.

Although you can vote when you're eighteen, you're not allowed to be a candidate in an election until you're twenty one. You don't have to be in a political party to stand for election – but most successful candidates are.

Using your representatives
You can do more than vote in elections though. The person elected represents you – whether or not you voted for him or her. Ask your representatives for help and advice, ask them what they think on particular issues and let them know your opinions too. If they want to get re-elected they can't afford to ignore you (if they do, write about it to your local paper). Find out the names and addresses of your representatives from your library, get to know the things for which each one is responsible and:
■ write them letters asking their opinions or giving yours
■ visit their advice surgeries (usually advertised in local papers)
■ invite them to public meetings
■ ask them to help (if you're having problems with officials for instance).

Influencing unelected officials

This is a much less straightforward business. Sometimes you'll be able to enlist the support of your MP or Councillors (it's always worth a try) but what if the problem's with the things *they* run? You may have problems with:

■ town hall officials
■ civil servants
■ health service administrators.

There *is* an official who can investigate problems of unjust treatment or bad administration by government and the health service – the Ombudsman. The snag is, only an MP or Councillor can ask for your case to be taken up!

What you have to try and do is try and get the interest of your representatives and the media. Though you may get somewhere on your own, you're more likely to get results by working with other people. Look at the following sections on p?rties, pressure groups and community action to see how you might be able to publicise and campaign for your case.

Influencing the education system

It can often seem that all sorts of people decide what, when and how you learn in schools or colleges without ever asking you what you think about it. Often the only choice you're given is "take it or leave it" (and if you're under sixteen you've simply got to take it!) All schools and colleges in the public sector have a board of governors and though they won't get involved in the day to day running of things, they can be used as a channel of influence. Most governors are appointed by local councils but since 1980 the numbers of parent governors in schools have risen and a few even have pupil governors. Make sure they know your views. In colleges, student governors are rather more common – usually chosen through the student union. The head teacher or principal is responsible to the governors.

If you're an individual you may not have much power but you can often get better results by joining with others. Get involved in your student union – make sure it represents your views. If your school doesn't have a School Council, suggest one should be set up to represent your interests.

Influencing your employer

Unless you're working for yourself or in a co-operative, your work contract gives someone else the right to decide what you do in return for paying you money. In the case of limited companies, your bosses take decisions which are intended to benefit the company shareholders and make a profit rather than benefit the company's workers. Unless you're a shareholder, you have no *right* to have your views listened to. Most employers will, however, consult and listen to their workers – through suggestion schemes, discussions with trade unions and informal contacts. Don't be afraid to give your views – good communication (on both sides) should make for fewer problems. If there are disagreements, use your union to represent your interest (see Chapter 2, *Working for a wage*).

Influencing businesses

You might want to do this because:
- someone plans to build a factory or processing plant next door to you
- someone is thinking about closing down one of the town's big employers
- you don't agree with a company's links with particular foreign countries
- you believe they are conducting cruel experiments
- you want the company's help for a community activity.

Since companies have an image to consider, they'll sometimes listen to the views of outsiders (especially people living nearby) but their real concern is with business. This means that if letters or meetings don't produce success, all you can do is boycott their goods or services and try and get other people to do the same. This sort of campaign is sometimes successful – but it's hard to keep going.

Political parties

Parties are groups of people who hold broadly similar views who work together to win (or keep) the power to govern the country according to their ideas. To do this they:
- select and support candidates for various elections and try to get their supporters to serve on various committees

■ develop and propose clear sets of policies to voters and try to
   attract their support.

The most important parties make sure that candidates supporting
their views stand in all elections. These are:

■ the Conservative Party
■ the Labour Party
■ the Alliance (Liberal Party and Social Democratic Party)

In Scotland and Wales the nationalist parties of Plaid Cymru and the
Scottish National Party (SNP) are also important while the party
system in Northern Ireland is very different – reflecting the fact that
a large minority of the population there don't want to be part of the
UK at all. Addresses of major parties are given in the final section
Making contact.

In addition there are a whole range of small parties – ranging from
the Ecology Party to parties of the far left (like the Communist
Party and Socialist Workers Party) and the far right (such as the
National Front and British Movement).

If you want to find out more about what the different parties
stand for, the best way is to contact the national address for
information and ask for contacts at local level. If you find that you
sympathise with most of the policies of one or other party, you may
want to join. Parties are always glad to have new members. You
don't have to agree blindly with absolutely everything the party
believes – just support its broad approach and most important
policies rather than those of the others.

Once you've been accepted as a member of your local branch,
you pay a yearly subscription and then there's usually as much (or as
little) activity as you want. You can:

■ help the party during elections (putting leaflets into envelopes,
   putting up posters, canvassing people's opinions door to door).
■ raise funds (dances and discos, coffee mornings, jumble sales,
   bingo sessions . . . the list could be endless).
■ join in discussions on policies (both to learn more and to help
   develop new ideas).
■ get signatures for petitions.
■ pass on your views to councillors and MPs.

None of these activities may sound particularly interesting to you,
but to the people involved they're seen as the "bread and butter" of
politics – what goes on in parliament and council chambers depends
on this work. If you do this sort of political work you may be trying

to get noticed so that you get picked to stand for election yourself –
but it's probably more likely that you're doing it with a sense of
purpose. Party workers really believe that what they do is useful and
important and enjoy working with others who share their values
with the same sort of dedication.

There are also sections especially for women members and young
members.

Pressure groups

These differ from political parties in that they are usually concerned
with a smaller range of issues, don't take part in elections for
councils or parliament in normal circumstances and don't want to
form a government.

They're groups of people with similar interests or views who've
joined or started an organisation to try and win support for their
concerns from the government, parties and public. Groups come in
all sizes and types. Some are local, some national and some
concerned with foreign countries. Some are concerned with a single
issue and nothing else while others try to represent their members'
interests on all sorts of topics. Some will fade away once their
objective is achieved (or lost), others are permanent organisations.
Just as the purposes and set-up of groups varies, so do the ways in
which they work – it's impossible to generalise and the whole field
is changing all the time as new issues emerge.

Joining a pressure group gives you the chance to influence people
all the time (not just at elections) and increase your interest in the
issues which really concern you – whether they are peace, the
environment, animals, political prisoners, disability, race relations,
transport, education or young people.

There isn't really any one single up-to-date guide to pressure
groups but some of the most active ones are listed in *Making contact*
(below). Your library should be able to give you details of any active
in your area and suggest specialist places to look.

Community action

This is a term which describes a kind of practical local politics which
isn't based on party lines but on participation and action. By acting
with others in your neighbourhood, you can sometimes get things

done (or stop things being done) by influencing businesses or government to change or reverse policies. You can also do things for yourselves. Community action is an approach which tries to take politics out of town halls and committee rooms and bring it back to people in the streets and in their homes. There are no central organisations and groups get born, die, change direction and merge as people's interests develop. Even so, things get done and if you get involved you'll probably get excited about the potential. Community action is about projects like:

- creating jobs on run–down estates
- providing services like shops for isolated rural areas
- improving play facilities for local children by building adventure playgrounds
- setting up clubs for young people, mums and toddlers, pensioners
- producing community newsletters and magazines
- clearing up waste ground and turning it into a park
- arguing to keep a threatened bus route
- painting wall murals to brighten up the area
- running festivals simply to have fun.

Profile

"There's absolutely nothing in our village for people to do in the evenings – there's not even a pub for two miles. Loads of people used to get the bus into town for the evening but then they said we were being cut to three buses a day – and the last one back was going to be at 8.30. It would have been dreadful if they had got away with it so me and a couple of friends drew up a petition and got almost everyone to sign it. Our councillor heard about it and decided to help us and told the local paper. With a bit of help we got the bus company to back down."

Lenny, 19, (Shop assistant)

If you feel there's a need to do something in your neighbourhood, don't sit around waiting for someone else to do something – do it yourself! Politics is too important to be left to politicians.

Making contact

Political parties

Conservative Party, 32 Smith Square, London SW1P 3AH. Tel: 01 222 9000.

Labour Party, 150 Walworth Road, London SE17 1JT. Tel: 01 703 0833.

Liberal Party, 1 Whitehall Place, London SW1A 2HA. Tel: 01 839 0492.

Plaid Cymru, 51 Heol yr Eglwys, Gadieriol, Cardiff

Scottish National Party, 6 North Charlotte Street, Edingburgh

Social Democratic Party, 4 Cowley Street, London SW1. Tel: 01 222 7999.

Pressure groups

The following list can't even attempt to be comprehensive – or even balanced, but it does list some of the most active, influential and long-lasting groups. Use your library to find details of others.

Amnesty International, Tower House, 8–14 Southampton Street, London WC2. Tel: 01 836 5621. Campaigns for all non-violent political prisoners.

Animal Aid, 111 High Street, Tonbridge, Kent. Works to abolish all animal experiments.

Anti-Apartheid Movement, 89 Mandela Street, London W1P 2DQ. Tel: 01 580 5311. Campaigns against racial segregation and discrimination in South Africa.

British Union Against Vivisection, 143 Charing Cross Road, London WC2. Tel: 01 734 2691.

British Youth Council, 57 Chalton Street, London NW1 1HU. Tel: 01 387 5882. Representative forum for most youth organisations in Britain. Pressures on youth affairs, tries to develop local youth councils.

Campaign for Homosexual Equality, BCM CHE, London WC1N 3XX. Works to end discrimination against gay men and women.

Campaign for Nuclear Disarmament, 11 Godwin Street, London N4. Tel: 01 263 4954. Campaigns to try and get rid of nuclear weapons.

Child Poverty Action Group, 1 Macklin Street, London WC2B 5NH. Tel: 01 242 3225. Anti–poverty group.

Community Relations Councils. There are dozens of these groups throughout the country which exist to fight racial discrimination. Send for a list from the Commission for Racial Equality, Elliot House, 10–12 Allington Street, London SW1E 5EH. Tel: 01 828 7022.

Disability Alliance, 25 Denmark Street, London WC2A 8NJ. Tel: 01 240 0806. Campaigns for disabled people – members include many other groups for people with disabilities.

Disablement Income Group, Attlee House, 28 Commercial Street, London E1 6LR. Tel: 01 247 6877. Seeks to improve living standards for disabled people.

Friends of the Earth, 377 City Road, London EC1V 1NA. Tel: 01 837 0731. Concerned with conservation, re-cycling, safe energy and combatting pollution.

Gingerbread, 35 Wellington Street, London WC2 7BN. Tel: 01 240 0953. Self-help group for single parents.

Help the Aged, 8–10 Denman Street, London W1A 2AP. Tel: 01 437 2554.

Hunt Saboteurs Association, PO Box 19 London SE22 9LR.

National Council for Civil Liberties, 21 Tabard Street, London SE1. Campaigning for people's rights under the law.

National Society for the Prevention of Cruelty to Children, 1 Riding House Street, London W1P 8AA. Tel: 01 580 8812.

National Trust, 42 Queen Anne's Gate, London SW1H 9AS. Tel: 01 930 1841.

National Union of Students, 461 Holloway Road, London N7 6LJ. Tel: 01 272 8900.

Oxfam, 274 Banbury Road, Oxford. Tel: (0865) 56777.

Royal Society for the Prevention of Cruelty to Animals, The Causeway, Horsham, Sussex RH12 1HG. Tel: (0403) 64181.

Shelter, 157 Waterloo Road, London SE1. Tel: 01 633 9377. National campaign for the homeless.

War on Want, 467 Caledonian Road, London N7 9BE. Tel: 01 609 0211. Seeks to fight the causes of poverty in Britain and the Third World.

Youthaid, 9 Poland Street, London WC1V 3DG. Tel: 01 439 8523.

Some have local branches, others don't. Some need your practical help, others are research or information bodies you can use.

9. Mind and body

Health care ■ staying healthy ■ disability
■ drugs ■ sex and the law ■ VD ■ birth control
■ if you're pregnant ■ parenting ■ gays
■ sexual assault ■ help and advice

Health care

The best form of health care is to prevent illness or accident as far as
you can by trying to live a healthy, safe life. Nevertheless, there will
probably be times when you need expert help. The National Health
Service was set up to make health care available to everyone,
regardless of their income. Today, however, there are charges for
prescriptions, for dental treatment or for glasses which you *may*
have to pay in addition to your National Insurance contributions if
you're working.

Doctors

Anyone over the age of sixteen can choose which doctor they want
to go to – but doctors can choose their patients too (though most
NHS doctors will take you unless they're full). If you don't like
your doctor or don't want to go to the same one as your parents you
can change. Do this by filling in part A of your medical card. This is
a card you'll have been given when you were born or became a
permanent resident in the UK. If you can't find yours, ask the local
Family Practitioner Committee (look it up in the phone book under
"F"). If you're new to an area it's probably best to ask someone if
they can recommend a good doctor but if you can't, contact the
Family Practitioner Committee (or look at main Post Offices) for a
list.

   If you're away from your home district for three months or less,
you can go to any local doctor for treatment – explain that you're a
temporary resident and give your NHS number (on your medical
card).

Dentists

Finding a dentist is like finding a doctor – ask around your friends and neighbours or try the Family Practitioner Committee, main library or Post Office. Whenever you go for dental treatment you should always say that you want NHS treatment (unless of course, you do want private treatment).

Dental check-ups are free and so is treatment (fillings and so on) in some cases. Otherwise, you have to pay for treatment. You can get it free if:

■ you're under eighteen (except for dentures or bridges if you're not in full-time education).

■ you're under nineteen and still in full-time education.

■ you're pregnant or have had a baby within the past twelve months.

■ you're getting certain other benefits (like family income supplement or supplementary allowance).

■ you've got a low income (in which case you should ask your dentist for form F1D, fill it in and post or take it to the social security office. They'll let you know if you qualify for free treatment). Exactly what counts as a "low income" depends on all sorts of things. Look at form D.11 (available from most post offices or the DHSS) for guidance and *claim anyway* – there's nothing to lose.

Glasses

If you're getting headaches or blurred vision, consult your doctor – it may be something more than your eyes that are wrong. If you simply want a sight test, you can get one free of charge on the NHS. Most opticians will do this test and examine your eyes. You will be prescribed glasses if needed and can get them either from the place which tested your sight or any other optician.

The law has just changed so you'll probably have to pay. You'll definitely have to pay if you want contact lenses.

Prescriptions

NHS prescriptions cost £2 per item at present but some people can still get them free. You'll be able to if you're:

■ under sixteen

■ an OAP

■ pregnant or have had a baby within the last twelve months

- suffering from one of several special conditions
- claiming benefits like family income supplement or supplementary allowance
- on a low income.

Look at form P.11 from most Post Offices and all DHSS offices for full details of who's eligible and how to claim (the methods vary).

Staying healthy

There's plenty you can do to keep yourself healthy. This section looks at just three areas: *diet, exercise* and *avoiding stress*.

Diet

Lots of people follow special diets all the time as part of the way they live for:
- religious reasons (Jews and Moslems for example)
- moral reasons (for instance many vegetarians and vegans)
- medical reasons (diabetics, people with allergies and so on).

Other people use special diets as a short–term way of controlling their weight. If you're careful about what you eat and drink normally, you shouldn't need to do this – a diet should be a permanent programme for healthy eating, not a one–week wonder. Most people in Britain could improve their diet by:
- *Cutting down on*: sugar, cakes and biscuits, salt, fats and oils.
- *Eating more*: fresh vegetables, fresh fruit, fish, non–fatty meats, wholemeal bread.

If you can do this it'll mean you'll probably be better nourished, keep your own teeth, have a better complexion, be less prone to obesity (being overweight) and have less chance of a heart attack in later life. Just about all bookshops will have a shelf full of books on healthier eating.

Although a lot of people *are* overweight, many more worry about being too fat when they're not. This worry can lead you to starve yourself – an illness called *anorexia nervosa* which can be extremely serious, especially as sufferers may not believe there's anything wrong with them. You should get medical advice if you're worried about anorexia, or contact one of the groups listed in *Help and advice*.

Exercise

Lots of people are so unfit that they're out of breath after running for a bus, climbing steps or carrying heavy shopping. If you don't want to feel old before your time, you should think about taking regular exercise as a way of staying fit. It needn't cost anything:

- walking
- gardening

- jogging and running
- cycling

are all free.

Chapter 11, *Time out*, has more details of sport and physical recreation opportunities.

Avoiding stress

This is when your mind and body feel tense, uneasy and unsettled. It's a common complaint in today's society and can make you more prone to serious illnesses like heart attacks and ulcers as well as accidents at home, at work or on the roads.

Not all stress is bad – life would be extremely boring without some challenges, it only becomes serious when you feel pressured *all the time* by things like:

- problems at work or college
- financial worries
- loss of a job and unemployment
- splitting up with a partner
- the death of someone close to you.

Exactly how these things affect different people isn't clear – some people are able to tolerate (or even enjoy) levels of pressure which others find too much to take. One thing that seems to matter is the amount of support you have from other people – the more isolated you feel, the more likely it is that stress will become a problem. Symptoms of stress may include:

- inability to sleep
- depression
- regular indigestion
- problems in concentrating
- sexual difficulties
- feeling guilty about relaxing
- aches and pains
- sudden loss of temper.

If you're worried that you're over-stressed, consult your doctor. If you want to keep it at bay, find out about ways of relaxing and unwinding such as yoga, massage or meditation (your library should have books on these). You could also try exercise – many people find that this helps. Finally, *make* yourself sit down once or twice a day for five or ten minutes and *do nothing*. If you can avoid falling asleep you're likely to find that it refreshes you for the next part of the day and stops you feeling so tense.

Disability

Almost everything in *Help Yourself* applies to people with disabilities just as it does to able bodied people but it's also worth mentioning a few of the special schemes and services to help you if you're disabled. Of course, one of the biggest problems faced by disabled people is the often patronising and prejudiced attitudes of the able bodied – but it's education rather than information which will solve this. The more opportunities you take, the more barriers can start to be broken down.

You'll know already how your disability affects your life and how you can cope with the difficulties it presents. You're also likely to be aware of various self-help groups or societies – either for all disabled people or just for those with your sort of disability. There may well be others though, of which you've not heard — for more information, use *Compass – Direction Finder for Disabled People* (price £2.25 plus 50p post and packing, available from DIG, Attlee House, 28 Commercial Street, London E1 6LR.) or *Directory for the Disabled* by Ann Darnborough and Derek Kinrade (price £5.50, from bookshops or RADAR, 25 Mortimer Street, London W1N 8AB. Tel: 01 637 5400.)

Employment

Contact the Disablement Resettlement Officer (DRO) through your local Jobcentre or Employment Office for details of special assessment, training and employment schemes as well as different rules concerning your eligibility for other schemes like YTS and TOPS. You may also be able to get help with your fares to work.

If you register as disabled at the Jobcentre (this is not the same as registering with your local council) you may become eligible for other help and your employer will be able to count you towards the "quota" of disabled people which all large firms should, by law, employ. Ask for leaflet DPL1 for details.

When job-hunting, you may find it helpful to be able to explain to employers what assistance they could get in employing you. Look at leaflet EPL71 *Aids and Adaptations*. Details of other leaflets available from the DRO are given in *Help and advice* below.

Entertainment and leisure

It's best to contact places in advance to check what facilities are available or could be provided – some places may not make any effort at all but others will do their best to help. Fire regulations in some cinemas and theatres may mean wheelchair users must be accompanied by an able bodied person.

Increasing numbers of theatres and halls are installing induction loop or help (including signing) for deaf people. Check also for wheelchair access and special loos – in older buildings especially these can be real problems.

Ask your local council about concessions for sports facilities like swimming pools and use tourist boards as well, particularly for details of places to stay on holiday. The London Tourist Board produces a very useful guide *London for the Disabled Visitor* (price £0.95 from bookshops or at 30p extra for post and packing from the Board, address in *Help and advice*.)

Sex

For advice, counselling and information on all personal and sexual matters, contact SPOD (Association for the Sexual and Personal Relationships of the Disabled, address in *Help and advice*).

Transport and travel

A really helpful booklet, *Door to Door* is available free from the Department of Transport, 2 Marsham Street, London SW1. Covers everything from learning to drive, makers' discounts on cars, fare concessions and help with road, sea rail and air transport.

Education

The National Bureau for Handicapped Students is a central point which can provide information and advice (details in *Help and advice*). You should also see if the colleges to which you've applied have a staff member responsible for advising disabled students. Make sure to discuss any special needs – colleges are increasingly prepared to do their best to help (although you're bound to find a few that don't) with things like readers, ramps and so on. Probably one of the biggest problems is likely to be wheelchair access – and split-site colleges. Even with the best will in the world there may be considerable difficulties here.

If your disability means you aren't able to attend college, you can still study through distance learning – either correspondence courses or through the Open University which has its own Disabled Student's Adviser. Get more details from the OU, Wilton Hall, Milton Keynes, MK7 6AA. Tel: (0908) 74066. In addition, look at *Second Chances for Adults* – details at the end of Chapter 6.

Welfare benefits

A variety of special welfare benefits are available to disabled people. The rules and regulations can get very complex. Look at leaflet HB1 from main Post Offices and any Department of Health and Social Security Office. This is called *Help for Handicapped People* and outlines the support available from a variety of sources: central government, local social services, housing departments and voluntary organisations. There's also the annual *Disability Rights Handbook* (price £2.20, post-free published by the Disability Alliance, 25 Denmark Street, London WC2A 8NJ. Tel: 01 240 0806). A thorough and comprehensive guide.

Drugs

The word *drug* means any substance used in a medicine or which affects your nervous system in some way. Drugs can pick you up or slow you down, make you relaxed or sleepy, alert or active. They can kill pain or may make your senses work overtime, make you feel good or kill you.

As well as using drugs to treat illnesses, people have, for centuries, used them simply for pleasure or to help them forget their problems. Despite this history there's still a lot of fear and ignorance surrounding drugs – and to some extent the law confuses things: One or two of the drugs which it's illegal to use or possess without a doctor's prescription are probably no more dangerous than those you can buy in any supermarket.

Legal drugs

One mild drug many people take at least once a day is caffeine.

Found in coffee, it acts as a stimulant – that's why some people drink strong black coffee to help them stay awake or wake up. A few people *do* get dependent on caffeine but no-one's suggesting that coffee drinking is a big social problem. But with other legal drugs that's not the case; there are two in particular which are known to cause thousands of deaths but which are still freely available – these are tobacco and alcohol.

Smoking tobacco is a widely accepted habit, even though it's clear that it contributes to more than 50,000 premature deaths every year through cancers, strokes, bronchitis and heart attacks. If you smoke when pregnant, your baby is more likely to be premature and underweight than if you don't. Although it's clear that many smokers begin the habit to imitate their friends, it's not always clear what it does for you. Some people say it keeps them alert, others say it helps them relax. Whatever the reason, it's now obvious that the benefits are far fewer than the dangers. As well as risking addiction to the poison nicotine, smokers also inhale tar into their lungs.

An even more widely used recreational drug is alcohol (going out for a drink is a favourite activity for many of us). Small quantities of alcohol with food help the digestion and some red wine can *reduce* your chances of heart attacks. In addition, a drink can certainly help you unwind after a hard day. The problem however, is that lots of people drink more than is good for them.

Drinking too much simply makes you drunk – your speech is slurred, you get clumsy, may feel dizzy or sick and want to fall asleep. Afterwards you may have a hangover for most of the following day with sickness and headaches (plenty of fruit juice is a good remedy). Being drunk isn't much fun and you often end up doing and saying things you regret later – which makes you feel worse. In particular, driving when drunk is senseless as you can put other people's lives in danger as well as your own.

Although your body can probably cope with the occasional binge (but watch out if you're taking any kind of pills or medicine) it can't handle prolonged heavy boozing. You could be in danger of joining Britain's three quarters of a million alcoholics and problem drinkers.

Exactly what "too much to drink" means can vary from person to person. Since some drinks are stronger than others, experts don't talk about numbers of drinks but numbers of "units". A unit is either:

■ a half pint of beer or
■ a glass of wine or
■ a glass of sherry, martini or port or
■ a single measure of spirits.

The Health Education Council says that men drinking more than twenty units per week and women drinking more than thirteen units start running the risk of harming themselves. Men drinking more than fifty units and women drinking more than thirty five units a week are very much in danger.

Alcoholism, which can either mean a physical or mental dependence on drink, leads to liver damage, stomach disorders, obesity and brain damage. People with a drink problem are also more prone to psychological problems like depression. It can also cause temporary impotence in men. If you drink when you're pregnant, the weight of your baby will be affected and if you're a heavy drinker, your baby's risk of physical deformity or mental handicap will be higher.

When you're drunk your reaction times are slower – that's why drinking and driving can be dangerous even when you don't realise it. Over half of all drivers in fatal accidents have alcohol in their bloodstream. The most sensible thing to do is to avoid drinking and driving entirely – but if you must, stay legal. An *average* man will be just inside the legal limit on 5 units and an *average* women on 3 units. This may be too much if you've been drinking earlier in the day – or even the previous day.

Despite the proven dangers of alcohol and tobacco, they're both perfectly legal. People who make these drugs also make high profits – and the government benefits by taxing you when you buy them (more than £4.5 million a year is raised on alcohol alone).

If you want to stop smoking, try your doctor for advice or contact Action on Smoking and Health (ASH), 5–11 Mortimer Street, London W1N 7RJ. Tel: 01 687 9843.

If you have a drink problem, contact your doctor. You may also want to get support from Alcoholics Anonymous – a self-help organisation of others who have been through problem drinking. There are local groups throughout the country. Get details from your local library or contact: AA, 11 Redcliffe Gardens, London SW10 9BG. Tel: 01 352 9779.

Prescribed drugs

Many drugs which are prescribed by doctors for common problems can lead to addiction and become harmful if used over an extended period. This is particularly true of tablets prescribed for stress or as sleeping pills.

Illegal drugs

There are all sorts of drugs which it is illegal to possess or use without a prescription. The law puts them into three classes: A, B and C. The ones in class A are supposed to be the most dangerous and the ones in class C the least – although some experts feel not all drugs are in the right category. Penalties for having these drugs also vary according to the class they're in:

■ Class A includes: Heroin, cocaine, morphine, LSD ("acid") and PCP ("Angel Dust").
■ Class B includes: Amphetamines, cannabis ("hash/dope/grass/ marijuana") and benzedrine.
■ Class C includes: Mandrax.

People take illegal drugs for the same sorts of reasons that they smoke or drink – to make them feel good. There's also curiosity – to find out what the fuss is about and sometimes some people get a thrill out of breaking the law.

Some illegal drugs (such as cannabis) are not known to be addictive nor particularly harmful and are acceptable to many people, other drugs like heroin are extremely dangerous and addictive. The law may be inconsistent about what's allowed and what isn't – but the real point is that all drugs are bad for you in excess (and yes, that even includes coffee!) and most illegal ones *are* dangerous, expensive and difficult to give up once you've started.

Find out more

Whether they're legal or illegal, you should find out more what particular drugs can do to your mind and body *before* you're tempted to experiment. Look at:

■ *Well being – helping yourself to good health*, edited by Robert Eagle, Penguin Books, £1.95. Has a readable section on all sorts of addictions.
■ *Alternative London*, edited by Georganne Downes, Otherwise Press, £3.50. Streetwise section on drugs. Gives all the facts so you can make up your mind.

The law
The police can stop and search you if they believe you've got illegal drugs. See Chapter 7 (*Rights and laws*) for more information. It's also against the law to allow your premises to be used for drug taking and dealing in drugs; even if you're only supplying friends, you could end up with a prison sentence.

Sex and the law

Some people would say that the law should not interfere with what you and your partner are happy to do in private. Other people say that the law must protect people who could be harmed by sex and also enforce particular moral standards. You may hold either view or else agree with some parts of the law but not others. To know what you're talking about however, you need the facts. There are many laws concerning sex (ones concerning prostitution and pornography for instance) but this section only looks at two: the age of consent and the law concerning homosexuality.

The age of consent
Any male having sex with a girl before she's sixteen breaks the law. The fact that she may have agreed to it is no excuse, the law says she's too young to consent to sex. Girls who have under age sex don't break the law – only the man can be prosecuted (as long as he's at least fourteen). Only if the girl was over thirteen and the man under twenty four can he defend himself by saying he didn't know she was under age.

A boy can have sex at any age – there's no age of consent. Although a woman can't be prosecuted for sex with an under aged boy, she could be charged with indecent assault if he's under sixteen.

Only men can be prosecuted for rape or attempted rape but both men and women can be prosecuted for incest (see *Sexual assault* below).

Even if a woman is over the age of consent she can still face problems until she's eighteen. Social workers may try to take into care under-eighteens who they believe to be "in moral danger". This can be because they think you're at risk of getting involved with prostitution, because they think you're sleeping around – or even because they think you shouldn't be sleeping with your boyfriend (this is rare unless he's considerably older than you).

Homosexuality and the law

If you're a man under the age of twenty one, any kind of homosexual activity is illegal – even if you and your partner want it. Once you're over twenty one it's legal only:

■ IF your partner is over twenty one too
■ IF you're in England, Scotland or Wales (it's still illegal at all times in Northern Ireland)
■ IF neither of you is in the armed forces (where it's still a crime)
■ IF it's in private (that can mean no-one in the same flat, house or hotel).

Even kissing in public could get you arrested and trying to pick up another man is also risky (it's an offence called "importuning").

If you're a woman things aren't so complicated – the law doesn't recognise such a thing as female homosexuality! Even so, women gays who display their affections openly in public may be stopped for "behaviour likely to cause a breach of the peace". Women gays with children may also face problems from social and welfare workers questioning their fitness as mothers.

The law discriminates against gay people but if you think this is wrong there are organisations which campaign to change things. Contact the Campaign for Homosexual Equality (see *Help and advice* for details).

Veneral diseases (VD)

These are diseases transmitted by intimate sexual contact. The law talks about three:

■ syphilis ("the pox")
■ gonorrhoea ("the clap")
■ chancre (pronounced "shanker" and not very common in Britain)

but there are other infections which are linked to sexual activity as well: herpes, thrush, trichomiasis and "non-specific urethritis" (NSU) for example.

The only way you can catch syphilis or gonorrhoea is by direct sexual contact with someone already infected – not from loo seats or door handles. You can get some of the other infections though without having had any sort of sexual contact with anyone at all.

All the diseases mentioned above can be cured (with the exception of herpes – which is like having occasional cold sores on

your sex organs. You can't get rid of it but your doctor can give you
ointment to relieve discomfort when you get attacks) but if you
think you may have VD get attention immediately. If left untreated
some diseases can have very serious consequences and you could
also pass on the infection to others.

The symptoms of these diseases vary considerably. Women in
particular may find it hard to know if they've got the disease since
none of the symptoms may be present. In addition having any of
these symptoms doesn't always mean you've got VD. All the same,
common symptoms of VD include:

- pain when you pee
- itching, soreness or rashes around your sex organs or anus
- any unusual discharge from your sex organs
- swollen glands in your groin.

If you're worried that you might have VD you should find out as
soon as possible either so you can stop worrying, or you can get
treatment to get back to normal quickly and you can warn your sex
partner or partners to get treatment and stop them passing it on to
others.

You can either see your doctor if you think you may have VD or
go to a special clinic for tests and treatment. These are based at most
big hospitals (look in the phone book under VD or "VENEREAL
DISEASES" for details). You don't have to make an appointment –
just go along when they're open. Treatment is free and confidential.

If you get VD it doesn't mean you're dirty or sleep around a lot.
Anyone who has sex with someone who isn't a virgin could catch it.
Some people feel ashamed if they get these diseases, even though
gonorrhoea is one of the most common contagious diseases after
measles! The only thing you *should* feel ashamed about is if you
know or suspect you've got the disease and pass it on to someone
else.

AIDS

This disease has been in the news a lot recently. It stands for
Acquired Immunity Deficiency Syndrome and is a relatively new
but growing problem. Although only one in ten people who come
into contact with the disease ever develop symptoms it's a serious
disease which can lead to death. What happens in simple terms is
that your body's defence systems stop working. At the moment
there's no known cure. The AIDS virus can be transmitted into

your blood in a variety of ways – but one way is through sex. AIDS can affect anyone but doctors are particularly worried about the extent to which it's carried between gay men who have been its main victims in this country so far.

Because of this problem, *all* gay men who have been sexually active have been asked not to give blood donations.

As with other sexually transmitted diseases, if you think you may be infected it's very unfair to have sex and risk passing on the infection. Symptoms of AIDS include:

■ weight loss
■ diarrhoea
■ skin problems
■ chest problems

Birth control

Anyone who is sexually intimate with someone of the opposite sex and doesn't want to become a parent is irresponsible if they don't think about this. Every year, unwanted, unplanned pregnancies and the fear of pregnancy bring unhappiness / and worry to thousands and thousands of women (and many men too). Much of this distress could be avoided if people thought about birth control.

Of course the easiest, cheapest and safest way to avoid pregnancy is not to have sex. Many people manage happily without it – so don't be pressured into thinking there's anything wrong with you if you want to wait.

The fact is however, that many people *do* enjoy sexual activity – wishing or pretending they don't and keeping them ignorant of birth control techniques is pointless and cruel.

Anyone over sixteen in Great Britain can get free, confidential advice from a special Family Planning Clinic (look in the phone book under "FAMILY PLANNING" for details). You can also ask your own doctor although not all will offer this service. At the clinic you can find out about the different methods of birth control, talk about them and find one which suits:

■ your body
■ your age group
■ your moral beliefs

You don't have to be married to go to a clinic and both women and men can get contraceptives free of charge.

If you are under sixteen
At the time of writing, doctors and clinics aren't allowed to give girls under sixteen birth control advice or prescribe contraceptives without their parents' or guardians' say-so (unless it's an emergency). This is the result of a recent controversial court ruling which *may* be changed. In the meantime, sexually active under aged girls cannot be stopped from using birth control methods which don't require prescriptions.

Natural methods of birth control
Some people's moral or religious beliefs mean that they choose not to use particular methods of birth control. Instead they try to avoid pregnancy by:

■ *The Rhythm method*: This involves not having sex on those days in the month when the woman is fertile and likely to become pregnant. It's not a very effective method since few women have an absolutely regular menstrual cycle – and in addition can be frustrating for you and your partner. If you do choose this method don't just go by the calendar ask your doctor or the clinic for advice on how to work out the fertile days (you may need to take temperature readings over quite a lengthy period).

   The fact that this method is called the "safe period" is rather strange since it's not a very safe way of avoiding pregnancy at all. About 25% of women who use this method alone will get pregnant each year.

■ *Withdrawal*: This is very simple. You have sex normally until the man is ready to have an orgasm but then he withdraws his penis before ejaculating. It's a method which can leave you both dissatisfied and can spoil your enjoyment of sex, it means the man has got to be trustworthy and it's also not very reliable. Sperm can leave the man's body before his orgasm. About one in five women who rely on this method alone will become pregnant within a year.

Other ways to avoid pregnancy you may have heard of which don't involve contraception are basically useless so don't rely on myths like:

■ having sex standing up
■ jumping up and down afterwards (women)
■ having very hot baths afterwards (women)
■ having very hot baths before (men).

Contraceptives

Some of these can only be obtained with a prescription, others are more widely available.

■ *Condoms*: These are thin rubber sheaths which are rolled onto the man's erect penis before sex. They stop his sperm entering the vagina. The advantages are that condoms are widely obtainable from chemists or machines in many loos (they cost 50p for two). You don't need a prescription to buy them and they're free from Family Planning Clinics. They're quite effective if the instructions are followed, can prevent VD infection and have no side effects. The disadvantages are that they can be damaged or split, they can interrupt your enjoyment of sex both before and afterwards and can get expensive if you're buying. If condoms are to be effective, the man must take responsibility for contraception. About 10% of couples who rely on this method alone will start a pregnancy within a year. If used with a spermicide (below) this rate will drop to under 4%.

■ *IUDs*: Also known as "the coil", this stands for "Intra-uterine device", a small object inserted into the woman's uterus by a doctor which prevents pregnancy. It's very effective and once fitted, can be virtually forgotten from day to day. The disadvantages are that IUDs must be fitted by a doctor and can cause pain and bleeding when first fitted. For this reason they are not often prescribed to young women.

  No-one knows exactly how IUDs work but they're very safe – only about 2% of women who use this method will get pregnant each year.

■ *The diaphragm*: This is a rubber dome which the woman inserts into her vagina before sex. It prevents sperm entering her womb. You have to get diaphragms (usually known as caps) on prescription through doctors or clinics but you're taught to fit and remove them yourself. In order to be effective, you have to use the cap with a spermicide (see below). The advantage of this method is that there are no side effects and you only need to think about it a few hours before you have sex – which is also the disadvantage! It can prevent spontaneous love-making as it needs to be inserted about three hours before you have sex and left in place for several hours after. In addition, you have to get it through a doctor.

Used with a spermicide, the cap is an effective contraceptive – about 2–3% of women who use it will get pregnant within a year.

■ *Spermicides*: These are chemical creams or foams available without prescription from chemists or family planning clinics which are put into the vagina and destroy sperm. If you use them, follow the instructions carefully – some brands aren't suitable for use with the diaphragm. On their own, spermicides aren't entirely reliable (about 12% of women who use them and nothing else will get pregnant within a year). Used with other contraceptives, they can be part of a reliable combination. The advantage is that they're easily available and safe to use. The disadvantages are that they can be messy and unless you get them from a Family Planning Clinic, can get expensive.

■ *The pill*: There are, in fact, lots of different birth control pills. What they all do is release chemicals into a woman's body which prevent the ripening and release of eggs from the ovaries. Pills are only available on prescription and must be taken regularly. The biggest advantage of the pill is that it's very reliable; in addition it regularises a woman's periods and prevent period pains. The disadvantages are that you must remember to take pills every day (the same time each day is best), if you miss a day you should not rely on your pills to prevent pregnancy – use another contraceptive as well for the remainder of the month. Another disadvantage of the pill is that it increases your risk of blood clots, tension, depression and some minor infections.

The pill is the single most effective form of contraception. Only 1% of women who use it get pregnant each year. To make sure it's effective, read the notes which come in the packet carefully.

If you think you're pregnant

One sign of being pregnant is that your monthly period stops (though light bleeding can occur in early pregnancy). But you can miss a period or be very late for other reasons too; tiredness, stress, dieting – or even worrying about it being late. If your periods are irregular anyway, you may not notice anything. Other signs of pregnancy include frequently feeling or being sick and tenderness of the breasts as well as putting on weight later.

If you've had sex with a man anytime since your last period (even if you thought it was safe) you could be pregnant. The way to find out is to have a test. You can buy test kits to do this yourself from chemists – but they cost about £5 or more each. If the test says you're not pregnant, check again a week later because they can be wrong. If it says you *are* pregnant then it's probably true. Doctors, Family Planning Clinics and some chemists can also do tests for you. So can Brook Advisory Centres (see *Help and advice*). Tests other people do are probably more likely to be accurate. You need to take a sample of urine from your first pee of the day to be tested. Use a *clean* jar with an airtight lid for the sample.

If you've missed two periods a doctor will be able to tell if you're pregnant by examining you.

Once you find that you are pregnant you've got to take decisions *quickly*. Unless you were planning to start a family you'll probably feel rather shocked, maybe scared too – but you've got to think about what to do next.

The first thing will usually be to talk to people about the choices open to you and how you feel. Tell the person who got you pregnant – if he's worth anything at all he should stick with you and give help and support when you need it; if he doesn't want to know, you're well rid of him as soon as possible. You may want to talk to friends, particularly if they're a bit older or more experienced than you. If you're still in education, talk to someone you respect on the college or school staff, especially if you want to carry on with your course. You may also want to talk with people like youth workers or ministers of your religion. Finally, there's your parents – not at the end of the list because they're not important but because telling them will probably be embarrassing for you, particularly if you're not married. If you're under sixteen or if you're living with them they'll have to be told before they find out anyway. Even if you're independent, you may still want to turn to them for advice. They may start by being even more shocked than you, but when that's passed many parents turn out to be very supportive.

If there's no-one you know to whom you feel you can turn, contact the British Pregnancy Advisory Service or in Northern Ireland, the Ulster Pregnancy Service (see *Help and advice*). You will be able to arrange to see a counsellor who won't push you into one decision or another – just help you work thinks out for yourself. You may hear of another organisation called "Life" which offers support when you're pregnant. Be warned that this is *not* a neutral organisation. They will always tell you to go through with your pregnancy. If that's what you want, fine, if you're not sure, don't waste your time.

The choices open to you are:

■ go through with the pregnancy and keep the baby, with or without the father's help. If this is what you want but can see problems ahead, contact your local social services department. (Look under your county or borough name in the phone book for details.)
■ go through with the pregnancy and have the baby adopted or fostered (although this can be extremely upsetting).
■ try and get an abortion.

Although you should listen to other people, the final decision must be yours – you're the one who's pregnant. Only if you're under sixteen will others be responsible – and even then they should take your views into account.

If you do decide to seek an abortion, go to your doctor *immediately*, the sooner it can be arranged, the safer and less upsetting it is for you. Explain why you feel unable to continue with the pregnancy. If the doctor agrees, you'll be sent to a specialist who must also agree before you can go to hospital for an abortion. If either one of these doctors says you can't have an abortion you can ask to see others. In some parts of the UK it can be very hard to get an abortion because of this. If you're experiencing problems or delays, contact the British Pregnancy Advisory Service quickly for help and advice. In Northern Ireland, where the law is different, contact the Ulster Pregnancy Service straight away.

Never attempt to end your pregnancy other than through a legal abortion. Other ways either won't work (drinking gin and very hot baths for example) or they could injure or kill you (such as poking anything into the womb). They're also illegal.

Parenting

Parenthood is likely to bring about the biggest changes in your life – whether you're a man or a woman. If you're going to be bringing up a child on your own, the job and the pressures will be even greater. Sometimes you will wonder why you ever bothered, but for the rest of the time your child or children will probably become one of the most important interests and reasons for activity in your life.

While you're pregnant
Follow your doctor's advice and try and go to ante-natal clinics if you can. Unless there are problems with your pregnancy you'll be able to carry on working if you've got a job until quite late on – your doctor will advise. Chapter 2, *Working for a wage*, explains your rights concerning maternity pay and your right to your job back after you've had your baby.

Whether or not you've been working you will probably be entitled to free dental treatment, prescription charges and also a Maternity Grant (see Chapter 4, *Claiming benefit* for details of where to find out more). If you're on supplementary benefit or family income supplement you'll often be entitled to free milk and vitamins too, even after your child is born.

As soon as you can, have a test to see if you're immune to Rubella (German Measles). This disease can seriously harm your baby if you catch it in the first three months of pregnancy. While you're pregnant you should also try to stop (or at least cut down) your drinking and smoking as these can damage the baby's growth.

Giving birth
If it's your first time, you'll probably be advised to have your baby in a hospital so that there's plenty of help on hand if there are any complications. While this may be a good idea, many parents feel that hospital births are a bit like a conveyor-belt system. Certainly in some hospitals you won't be given any say about how (or even when) you give birth – and in some, the father won't be allowed to be present even if that's what both of you want. Other hospitals are, however, rather more aware of you as an individual and realise that giving birth is something over which you should have some control. Ask your friends about the reputations of the different hospitals and try to insist on going to the one which seems best to you. You may choose to give birth at home, in familiar surroundings – it is your right. Your doctor will be able to recommend another doctor or midwife if he or she doesn't deliver babies.

Once your baby is born
You should make sure that you are claiming child allowance (ask for form CH.1 from your nearest DHSS office) since almost anyone responsible for bringing up children is entitled to this. If you're a

single parent, you may be entitled to more (ask for leaflet CH.11).

Within six weeks you must register the baby's birth and get a birth certificate. If you gave birth in a hospital, the Registrar may visit you soon after but if you had a home delivery, you should go to the Registrar of Births, Marriages and Deaths to get the formalities sorted out.

If you feel depressed and run down after giving birth don't be surprised – it's a common feeling, probably caused by hormone changes in your body and will often pass. If the feeling continues for more than a couple of weeks though, see your doctor.

Unless you want another baby straight away you should start thinking about birth control again since the belief that you can't get pregnant if you're breast-feeding isn't true.

Support

Bringing up a child may be harder than you or your partner ever bargained for and you may feel you can't cope. Don't be afraid to turn to your own parents and others in the same position for help and advice – it's a feeling most parents will have and by talking about it and sharing ideas, you'll probably learn how to manage. Some of the organisations listed in *Help and advice* may be able to offer support too.

Gays

Most people are sexually attracted to members of the opposite sex – but not everyone's heterosexual though. Some people are attracted to their own sex or people of both sexes. These are homosexuals or gays (women homosexuals are also called lesbians) and bisexuals.

Nobody knows for sure why some people are gay and others aren't. The chances are though, that you'll probably know quite a few gay people – homosexuals come from all sorts of backgrounds and only a minority match the stereotypes we see in the media. Serious estimates suggest that between one in ten and one in twenty people are gay – you may be gay yourself. The thing is, that not everyone who's gay wants other people to know about it – some gays may even deny it.

This is because society and some groups within it believe that homosexuality is shameful and wrong. It needn't necessarily be like that though – in ancient Greece, for example, homosexuality was quite acceptable, even fashionable! Our society tolerates gays in a few ways but not in many others (see *Sex and the law* above) and this means that being gay isn't easy. You may face discrimination, ridicule, rejection by so-called friends and even violence if people know you're gay. Some gays choose to hide their feelings, they may even try to settle down with someone of the opposite sex to "cure" themselves, believing homosexuality is some sort of illness – which it certainly isn't.

"Coming out" (telling people you're homosexual) is a big decision and you may want help and advice about how to handle it. As well as talking to people you trust in your own community, you might also want to contact:

- *Gay Switchboard*, Tel: 01 837 7324. Open 24 hours. Confidential advice and information for gay men and women. Details of groups, meeting places and help throughout the country (and especially in London). Even if they can't help they should be able to give you details of who can.
- *Lesbian Line*, BCM Box 1514, London WC1N 3XX. Tel: 01 837 8602. (2pm to 10pm, Monday and Friday, 7pm to 10pm Tuesday and Thursday). Telephone information and support service for lesbians.
- *Icebreakers*, BM Gay Lib, London WC1N 3XX. Tel: 01 274 9590. (7.30 to 10pm except Sundays). Telephone information and support service for gay men who want to "come out".

As part of coming out, you may want to meet other gay men and women. Most large towns and cities have gay clubs and pubs – some aren't very friendly and are just pick-up points; they don't appeal to everyone. You may prefer a less commercial scene – and there are lots of less intimidating groups or societies. Wherever you live, try Gay Switchboard for details.

Remember though that your sexuality is only one aspect of your personality – don't neglect the others. You don't have to lose heterosexual friends or drop activities just because you're gay.

If you're not gay and have a friend who tells you she or he is, don't feel that they have to stop being friends – they're still going to be the same as before – and even if they're the same sex there's no need to assume that they want you as a sexual partner.

See the section on *Help and advice* for details of other groups for gays, including ones which work to change the law.

Sexual assault

This is when a person is used for sexual purposes against her or his wishes. In almost every case, women or children are the victims and men the aggressors. Although the most serious assaults involve force or the threat of violence, visual assault (by flashers) or verbal assault (such as obscene phone calls) can also be very distressing.

Obscene calls

Put the phone down straight away – don't let the caller know how upset or disgusted you are, that may be what he wants. Tell the police – there may not be much they can do this time but they ought to be made aware of the problem. If you're being bothered repeatedly, ask British Telecom to have your calls intercepted by the operator or your number changed – they're meant to be fairly sympathetic. You may choose not to have your name or number put in the directory – and even if it is included, just put your initials and not your first name.

If you ever get an obscene letter through the post, take both the letter and its envelope to the police.

Flashers

Unless you're confident and strong enough to challenge the flasher, walk on and try not to react. As soon as you can, report the incident to the police. This time he may get away – but your report could help catch him.

Gropers

This can be a problem in crowded lifts or trains – and it's difficult to prove it was anything other than accidental. At the very least, move away and get out as soon as you can. If you're feeling up to it, go on the offensive and say loudly "watch where you're putting your hands" or grab the hand and say "why do you keep trying to touch me?" You're unlikely to be able to do anything more than humiliate the person though.

Rape and violent assault

Reporting a rape can be almost as distressing and disturbing as the attack itself. You may find the police insensitive and unsympathetic – and even if they're not, you'll have to answer upsetting questions.

If you've been raped:

■ contact a friend first and go to the police with her. If there's no-one around to whom you can turn, contact the Rape Crisis Centre on 01 837 1600 (24 hours). There are services outside London too, in most cities – if you haven't got details, ask the London service.

■ don't wash or change your clothes until you've been examined by a doctor or been to the police.

■ visit your doctor or a hospital after you've been to the police. Get treatment for shock and injury and checks for possible pregnancy or VD.

Rape isn't simply a physical attack – you may feel very disturbed for months afterwards. As well as talking to your doctor, you may find it helpful to talk to a trained counsellor – Rape Crisis Centres should be able to put you in contact.

A number of rapes never get reported; some women are too upset and even ashamed to talk about it publicly. To get a rapist convicted, you'll have to go to court. This will be an ordeal – you'll have to relive the experience in front of people who won't necessarily be sympathetic and there's also the risk that justice won't be done. It's understandable if you don't feel able to go through with this – but by showing your determination, you can help protect other women.

Incest

This is a sexual assault from a member of your immediate family – and a crime. Recent indications are that it's more common than has been suspected – it's just that most cases aren't reported. If you've been a victim, you may feel reluctant to tell anyone for fear of what may happen – but you shouldn't have to put up with it. Sometimes threatening to tell people will stop the problem developing. You may also want to talk about it confidentially. Contact the Albany Trust, 16–18 Strutton Ground, London SW1P 2HP. – it's a long established counselling service for all sexual problems.

Avoiding attack

Forget the stupid myths that "nice girls don't get raped" or that "she must have asked for it", they're wrong. Rape can happen to any woman – you're not only at risk out of doors and with strangers, many victims are attacked by people they know and in their own

homes. That said, you can reduce the risk by:
■ avoiding shortcuts through dark, lonely areas
■ keeping your home secure
■ watching who you invite into your home (including acquaintances)
■ declining lifts (especially from groups of men)
■ learning to defend yourself.
If you are attacked or threatened you'll have to use your judgement about running, yelling or fighting but try and get as good a description as you can of the attacker.

If you're scared of going out at night you shouldn't just stay in and feel secure – you should feel angry. See if any local women's groups are campaigning about it – read the local press and magazines like *Spare Rib* for what's happening.

Help and advice

Health
Most health centres, doctors' and dentists' surgeries and clinics will have a variety of free information like:
■ health service provisions and facilities (including DHSS leaflets)
■ local support groups for people with particular medical conditions
■ advice leaflets on everything from diet, fitness and the dangers of smoking to how to avoid heart disease and how to brush your teeth.
In some areas, leaflets may be available in ethnic minority languages.

The *Health Education Council* produces all sorts of free and priced publications on all sorts of topics such as mental health, diet, exercise and sex education. Contact it for a list or details of what's available for issues which concern you: *Health Education Council*, 78 New Oxford Street, London WC1A 1AH. Tel: 01 637 1881. In Scotland, contact the *Scottish Health Education Group*, Woodburn House, Canaan Lane, Edinburgh EH10 4SG. Tel: 031 447 8044. Most District Health Authorities of the National Health Service (in Scotland called Health Boards) have Health Education Units too, look them up in your phone book to see what they offer.

There are a growing number of women's health groups – to find out if there's one near you or to set one up, contact the *Women's Health Information Centre*, 52 Featherstone Street, London EC1. Tel: 01 254 9094.

There are a lot of national groups for sufferers of particular conditions. They offer information, advice and support and sometimes raise funds for research. Two examples of organisations offering help to people suffering from anorexia nervosa and their families are: *Anorexic Aid*, The Priory Centre, Priory Road, High Wycombe, Bucks. Tel: (0494) 21431. If you send a s.a.e. they can supply details of local groups and information about the condition. There's also *Anorexics Anonymous*, 24 Westland Road, London SW13. Tel: 01 748 4587 which offers appointments for free advice and counselling for sufferers. To find out details of other groups, look at the *Social Services Yearbook* published annually by Longman. Since it costs £25 it's one to check in the library! Also look at the *Sunday Times Self-Help Directory*, £3.95, published by Granada Publications and *Self-Help and the Patient*, £2.50, published by the Patients' Association, Room 33, 18 Charing Cross Road, London WC1.

Of the many books on health which are available, one which is particularly clear is *Well being: helping yourself to good health* by Robert Eagle, published by Penguin Books, £1.95.

Disability
Leaflets available from the Disablement Resettlement Officer at your Jobcentre or Employment Office include:
- *The Disabled Persons Register (DPL1)*
- *Assistance with fares to work (DPL13)*
- *Training Opportunities for Disabled People (TSDN121)*
- *Into work (EPL41)*

In addition to the many associations for people with particular disabilities there are also more general groups including:
- RADAR (the *Royal Association for Disability and Rehabilitation*), 25 Mortimer Street, London W1N 8AB. Tel: 01 637 5400. As well as co-publishing the *Directory for the Disabled* (above), RADAR acts as a co-ordinating body for other groups and campaigns for better provision for disabled people, provides advice, information and many useful publications.
- *Disablement Income Group*, Attlee House, 28 Commercial Street, London E1 6LR. Tel: 01 247 2128 (also local groups). As well as

publishing *Compass* (above), campaigns to improve welfare and benefits and provides advice.
- the *Disability Alliance*, 25 Denmark Street, London WC2A 8NJ. Tel: 01 240 0806. An umbrella organisation for dozens of groups concerned with disability. Produces the *Disability Rights Handbook* (above).
- SPOD (the *Association for the Sexual and Personal Relationships of the Disabled*), the Diorama, 14 Peto Place, London NW1 4DT. Tel: 01 486 9823.
- *National Bureau for Handicapped Students*, 40 Brunswick Square, London WC1N 1AZ. Tel: 01 278 3459. Practical advice and information for students with disabilities and their colleges.

Increasing numbers of tourist boards are producing information for people with disabilities – for example *London for the Disabled Visitor* (above) from the London Tourist Board, 26, Grosvenor Gardens, London SW1. Tel: 01 730 0791.

Drugs

In addition to sources mentioned in the section, try:
- *Release*, 1 Elgin Avenue, London W9 3PR. Tel: 01 289 1123 or (24–hour emergency number) 01 603 8654. For information, advice and counselling on drugs and the law.
- SCODA (*Standing Conference on Drug Abuse*), 3 Blackburn Road, London NW6 1XA. Tel: 01 328 6556. Can provide information on where to get counselling and help with drug problems.

Sex, birth control and VD

Two excellent books on these topics, written in a clear and sensible way are:
- *Make it Happy* by Jane Cousins, published by Penguin Books, £1.50.
- *Talking Sex* by Miriam Stoppard, published by Piccolo Books, £1.25.

But beware out of date information on contraception and birth control advice for people under sixteen.

In addition to your own doctor, the following organisations should be able to help:
- *Family Planning Information Service*, 27–35 Mortimer Street,

London W1N 7RJ. Tel: 01 636 7866. Free advice and information, also details of local clinics.

■ *Brook Advisory Service*, 153A East Street, London SE17 2SD. Tel: 01 708 1234. (Head office, also centres in several other major cities – check your phone book). Birth control and contraception advice and counselling, pregnancy testing and information.

■ *British Pregnancy Advisory Service*, Austry Manor, Wooten Wawen, Solihull, West Midlands B95 6DA. Tel: (05642) 3225. (Head office, many local clinics and centres – check your phone book). Counselling, advice and information on birth control, pregnancy and abortion. In Northern Ireland, contact the *Ulster Pregnancy Service*, 338A Lisburn Road, Belfast BT9. Tel: (0232) 667345.

■ For help in continuing a pregnancy if you are facing problems at home, contact your local social services or *Life*, 118–120 Warwick Street, Leamington Spa, Warks. CV32 4QY (also local groups). Remember, *Life* does *not* offer unbiased counselling about whether or not to continue a pregnancy.

Parenting

For help in preparing for parenthood, ask your doctor and see if your adult education service has any parenthood classes. In addition try:

■ *National Childbirth Trust*, 9 Queensborough Terrace, London W2 3TB. Tel: 01 221 3833 (also local groups). Classes, pamphlets and books.

To check you're getting all your rights, look at:

■ *Maternity Rights Handbook* by Ruth Evans and Lyn Durward, £3.95 published by Penguin Books.

If you're bringing up a child on your own, get support from:

■ *Gingerbread*, 35 Wellington Street, London WC2E 7BN. Tel: 01 240 0953 (many local groups – self help organisation).

■ *National Council for One Parent Families*, 255 Kentish Town Road, London NW5 2LX. Tel: 01 267 1361.

If you find parenting is getting too much for you and you're starting to feel aggressive towards your children, contact:

■ *Parents Anonymous*, 9 Manor Gardens, London N7. Tel: 01 263 5672. Confidential and sympathetic help.

Gays

In addition to the groups mentioned in the section, contact:

■ Campaign for Homosexual Equality, BM, CHE, London WC1N 3XX. Tel: 01 359 3973.

10. Shelter

Moving out ■ plan ahead ■ emergency shelter
■ what's available ■ where to find places
■ what to look for when renting ■ once you're in
■ your rights as a tenant ■ help for people with
low incomes ■ help and advice

Moving out

Sooner or later, almost everyone thinks about moving out of the
home in which they grew up. Sometimes it's prompted by a desire
for more independence, sometimes by rows, or job prospects or
education.

Once you're 18 or over (16 in Scotland) you can live where and
how you want but if you're younger and want to move you'll need
to understand the law:

■ If you're under 16, you can't normally leave home. People who
do will get taken back as soon as they are found. Only if there are
bad problems (such as violence at home) will you be able to
move out into care. If things are bad, ask your local Social
Services for help and advice.

■ If you're between 16 and 18 you can live independently from
your parents' or guardians' if they agree. If you leave without
their permission you could be reported to the police as a missing
person. So long as you're supporting yourself and not in any
kind of trouble you probably won't have to go back. Watch out
though if you're sleeping with someone (especially girls with
older men) or if your friends are known to the police – a court
could declare you "at risk" and send you home. If that happens,
ask a social worker for advice.

Before doing anything, weigh up the advantages and disadvantages
of moving. You may decide that staying put is the best bet for now.
In terms of cost, it's hard to beat living at home but if independence
matters more then go ahead and move out (if you can afford to).

Plan ahead

Once you've decided to move, the important thing is to try and avoid being left homeless – this means preparation, especially if you're making a fresh start in a new area. Your aim should be to fix up your new place before leaving the old one but if that's not possible, try and arrange for friends or relatives to put you up temporarily. If you have to do this, make sure it's for as short a time as possible since it can be a quick way of losing friends!

Moving home always costs more than you think – so make sure you've got as much cash saved as you can manage. You'll need it for extras to make the place comfortable (see *Once you're in* below) as well as things like rent in advance and deposits. You may want to move to a new area of the country, perhaps there may be more jobs or more to do. Remember though that places to live in South East England cost far more than elsewhere and that London prices are the most expensive. At the very least, visit places to check the prices and availability of places before you decide to move there.

Emergency shelter

If things go wrong and you end up on the street, you've got to move fast to make sure you don't have to sleep rough – if that happens you'll find it harder than ever to get on your feet again. If you've got any money, a bed and breakfast place will buy you a few hours to think out your next move. Larger towns and cities have YMCA or YWCA hostels too – but get there as soon as you can because they fill up quickly.

If you can't afford somewhere to stay and things are getting desperate, try the DHSS or local Social Services department. If they're shut, try the police. In bigger places they might be able to point you to emergency hostels, night shelters or reception centres. If you end up with nowhere to go and there isn't anything open (launderettes, waiting rooms etc.) then multistorey carparks will at least get you out of the open in bad weather.

Some people lose contact with family and old friends but don't let pride stop you from contacting them for help if you're unable to break out of a bad patch.

One group of people who may need emergency shelter in a hurry are women escaping violence or threatened violence in the home. If this happens to you, you'll probably find most help and sympathy from Women's Refuges if you can't go to friends. They may not publicise their locations (to protect the people there) but Social Services departments, Citizens' Advice Bureaux or the police should be able to put you in touch with the nearest refuge.

What's available?

What's best for you depends on your particular circumstances and budget as well as what you'd like.

Private landlords/landladies
About one in ten households are renting their homes from a private owner. Many people move into this sort of accommodation when they first set up on their own. It can range from single rooms or bedsits in someone's house where you share bathroom and kitchen facilities right through to self-contained flats or houses. In some "digs" the landlord or landlady may provide meals. Almost all places are furnished. Rents can be high since the owners are renting out the property to make money – but if you've got the cash you'll almost always be able to find somewhere fairly fast. This type of housing is getting less common nationwide so it's becoming more of a "sellers' market".

   Rent is usually paid monthly or weekly in advance and you may also have to pay a deposit in case of damage which will only be returned when you leave. Some places also want you to have references, from a bank, employer or college for instance. Your rights in this type of housing can be quite complicated – depending on the exact arrangements (see *Tenants' rights* below).

Sharing
In order to live cheaply, many people share rented housing with others – and if you're new to an area it can be a good way to get to know people. You can either team up with some friends or move into an existing set-up (see *Where to find places* below). Regardless of who you share with there will be times when you don't get along but you can cut out a lot of problems if you are all clear about how tasks and bills are to be shared. Make sure you agree how to organise things like cleaning, washing up and buying things like light bulbs and loo rolls. Whatever you decide, make sure you do your share so

that no one can moan about you. It's also helpful to sort out how people feel about others staying: your flatmates may resent people virtually living with you and not contributing to bills or your regular weekend guests who always drink the last of the milk.

If you do go into a shared place with others, take care if you are the person who's signed the rental agreement – you could end up responsible if your flatmates break it, get behind with the rent or move out. If at all possible, try and arrange a joint agreement in everyone's name – some owners won't like this since it's more work for them, especially if the people in the place change frequently. The same goes for services like electricity – if it's in one person's name, you'll probably find that paying into a common kitty *in advance* will discourage people from doing moonlight flits when the bill's due!

Council housing

There's not a lot of new council housing being built and now that some tenants can buy their homes, pressure for places is very high. There are waiting lists everywhere – but you can't even get on the list in many areas unless you've already lived in the district for quite a while. Some councils will let you put your name down when you're 16, others make you wait until you're 18 or even 21.

Places are allocated to those in greatest need according to a "points" system which can vary from council to council – but you do have the right to know what the policy is – so ask at your district or borough council's Housing Department. If you're on the list and your circumstances change (pregnancy or marriage for example), tell the council – it could improve your chances.

The council is only obliged to find somewhere to stay for people in "priority need" (this includes families with children, pensioners, pregnant women and some others) but some places do have a small quantity of single persons' housing. The only other alternative is if the council has a policy of offering its "hard to let" property to childless people. If you're prepared to live in often very poor conditions this might be worth it.

Finally, remember that council housing is virtually always *unfurnished*, but if you're out of work, have no furniture of your own and get a place then consult the DHSS (see below) although you won't get anything if you're single.

Buying your home

More than half of all households own or are buying their homes – and the proportion is rising – especially since council housing started to be sold off. Most people who buy do so with mortgages – special loans from building societies, banks or local councils.

In order to get a mortgage you must be at least 18 and able to convince whoever is lending the money that you can meet the monthly repayments. In practice, you need a steady job or to have been self-employed for about three years. Although lenders give preference to people who've been saving money with them, it does pay to shop around and ask several banks or societies what their "lending policy" is. They will normally lend single people a maximum of $2\frac{1}{2}$ times their yearly income. The amount they lend couples varies from place to place (twice the higher yearly income plus once the lower yearly income is common). Because London prices are so high they may lend more for property there. You don't have to be married to get a joint mortgage and increasingly places are starting to lend money to groups of more than 2 people (though you'll have to look harder).

At the moment it's rare to find somewhere that will lend the full price of a place – you may have to find as much as 10% of the cost yourself. In addition to this deposit you will usually have to find several hundred pounds for things like surveys and legal fees – buying somewhere isn't cheap! As with most borrowing, you have to pay back all you were lent – usually over about 25 years plus interest which is worked out in a complicated way. The good thing about mortgages however is that you get tax relief on the interest you pay – ask the lender to explain how this works.

Not everyone wants to own property – some people prefer other ways of living such as co-ops. Certainly not many people think about buying until they've been working for a few years – simply because they can't afford it. If there's a chance that you might want a mortgage in a few years time, there's a special savings scheme for first-time buyers involving cash grants and interest-free loans. Ask building societies and banks about the Home Loan Scheme.

Shared ownership

This is an arrangement under which you can part-own and part-rent your home. It's for people who want to buy but can't afford to pay the full price straight away. You start by buying a share of the property (25% or 50% or 75%) and renting the remainder – usually from a Housing Association or new town (much less commonly a private landlord or landlady). The rents are set at a fair level and you have the right to increase the share of the property you are buying as you can afford it. If you decide to move you sell your share to someone else. Full details of how to become a home owner in stages are given in the booklet *Shared Ownership* published by the Department of the Environment and available free from the Citizens' Advice Bureau or local councils' Housing Departments.

Housing Associations

These are organisations which rent out property (rooms, flats or houses) but aren't in it to make a profit. Although rents may be slightly higher than council housing, they're not as costly as privately rented places. Some are for special groups such as old people or single parents and they're not too common in smaller towns. You can find details in yellow pages under "H" and contact them for more information (you can apply to go on the waiting list of as many as will take you). The local council's Housing Department will also be able to tell you about any in your area.

Housing Co-ops

Similar to Housing Associations in that they're not run for profit, these are groups of people who've joined together to provide themselves with housing (sometimes a single building, sometimes a whole street). You pay a reasonable rent to the co-op and have a say in running the housing along with all the other people in it. This form of housing isn't too common in Britain yet and most co-ops have long waiting lists but if you've got plenty of time and energy and can find at least 6 other people interested in the idea, then you could start your own. For more information, contact the Federation of Housing Co-ops, 16 First Cross Road, Twickenham, or the National Federation of Housing Associations (Co-op Housing Officer), 30 Southampton Street, London WC2. Tel: 01 240 2771.

Short Life Housing

Sometimes councils or other organisations have property which is waiting to be improved or pulled down or near the end of its lease. Sometimes they'll let you use it at a very low rent until they need it. If you don't mind having to move frequently and can stand some fairly poor conditions then ask councils or housing associations if there's anything in your area.

Jobs with accommodation

Some jobs offer accommodation to go with them – it's fairly common in the hotel and catering industry and for quite a few caretaking jobs. The good thing is that it'll either be free or cheap, the bad thing is that if you stop working there you've got to move out – and even when you are working you've hardly any rights. Child care jobs with accommodation thrown in are often advertised in magazines like *The Lady*.

Hostels

Most large towns have hostels run either privately or by organisations such as the YMCA or YWCA (you don't have to be Young or Christian to stay in them). They offer cheap accommodation for rent but are usually rather institutional, with all sorts of rules. Some places are basically only for short–term stays of one or two nights but others let you stay virtually indefinitely. The worse hostels (almost always the ones run for profit) can be pretty grim – sleeping in dormitories or 'cubicles' and none too clean. On the other hand, the best can be good value for money – with a bedsit of your own and sharing bathroom and kitchen with a few other people (rather like college halls of residence). Popular ones often have waiting lists. Find them in the yellow pages under "Hostels" but remember there are all sorts of hostels – some are for people just out of prison, some for alcoholics – so don't expect to find a suitable one straight away.

Squatting

This is about making use of property standing idle and empty. In 1977 a law was passed which made legal squatting difficult – but it can still be possible. The good thing about squatting is that it's cheap and is a way of protesting about unused housing at a time when there's a housing shortage. The bad points are that places are often in poor condition and are usually only temporary.

If you're serious about squatting you'll need to do plenty of planning and preparation. If you do it on impulse you could well end up at the police station on a charge of breaking and entering!

For information about squatting, contact the Advisory Service

for Squatters, 2 St. Pauls Road, London N1. Tel: 01 359 8814.
Always phone first or write to them.

Where to find places

The grapevine
Probably the best way to find private rented accommodation is to
ask around – friends, workmates, people you meet at parties. Many
places are never advertised anywhere but get passed on by
recommendation. You may be surprised how many people know
of others who plan to move, or of people with spare rooms to rent,
or of flats to share.

Estate agents
Most of their work is with people buying and selling property but a
few deal in rented accommodation too. Often these are for rather
posh places beyond most people's budget – but if you're prepared to
search round you may find a few that manage cheap rented places.

Newspaper and magazine adverts
This is probably the best bet for rented places and shares if asking
hasn't got you anywhere. It's important to get the paper or mag as
soon as it comes out (with local papers that means the lunchtime
edition). Places often go very quickly so you can't hang around or
leave it until the following day. Even if you're not thinking of
moving immediately, get in the habit of reading the adverts in the
"Accommodation" section to get some idea of what's available and
what you can afford. If you go for a shared place and it seems OK,
you've got to try and make a good impression since there's almost
always competition.

Shop adverts
Cards in newsagents are often a good way to find bedsits or
lodgings in someone else's house. The problem is that they're often
taken by the time you follow them up. This means you've got to
check regularly – sometimes the shop writes the date the advert
went up on a corner of the card so you can avoid the ones that aren't
new. Remember, you can always put up an advert yourself asking
for a place.

Local radio
A few local radio stations have been experimenting with helping
listeners find flatshares – either by publishing weekly lists you can
drop in and collect (get there early) or by having a regular spot in
their programmes. If your station doesn't do this, try writing to the
programme controller or one of the presenters to suggest they give
it a try.

Accommodation agencies
These usually seem to see their job as helping landlords and
landladies find tenants rather than helping people find homes.
You'll find them in the yellow pages under "Accommodation –
Residential".

   You should not have to pay agencies anything just to register
with them or get addresses of places to look at. If they ask for a fee
for this (which isn't uncommon) it's probably illegal – so get a
receipt for any cash you hand over and ask the Citizens' Advice
Bureau if you should take them to court. You should only have to
pay anything if they fix you up with a place.

   Read carefully any tenancy agreement you sign with an agency
(you could sign away many of your rights). If you don't understand
what it means, get advice. Finally, if you think that the agency is
discriminating against you on the grounds of your race or sex then
you should take action because it's illegal. See the chapter on *Rights*
in this book.

What to look for when renting

Never agree to take accommodation until you've visited it and had
a chance to look around. Be sure to find out about:

Money
- how much rent you pay, how often you pay (weekly or
  monthly) and to whom (the owner, a collector, another tenant).
- how much you will have to pay in advance and whether there's a
  deposit to pay as well. Non-returnable deposits (or "key
  money") are illegal.
- whether the rent includes heating, gas, electricity, rates and so
  on (if not, find out whether there are meters or if you have to
  contact the gas and electricity boards yourself).

■ whether there are any additional charges (in blocks of flats "service charges" for cleaning and upkeep of communal areas or gardens are often common).

Once you've got the answers, ask yourself whether or not you can afford the place. This seems so obvious it's hardly worth saying – but all the same, many people end up having to move because they underestimated the costs involved. Think of all the costs involved and then look at how much money you'll have left over each month – even if you could afford it, you might decide you'd enjoy life more by taking somewhere cheaper and having extra money to spend.

Unless you pay rent weekly, you don't *have* to be given a rent book – but always get a receipt for any money you pay. If you can't get one, try to pay by cheque and keep your cheque stubs.

Contents

■ if the place is furnished, make sure you and the owner get together when you move in and make a list of *everything* provided (such as vacuum cleaners, furniture, bedding, even teaspoons). If anything is damaged, make sure that's noted. This list is called an inventory and both you *and* the owner should sign it. This means that your landlord or landlady can make you pay for anything lost or damaged but that you can't be held responsible for anything that's supposed to have gone missing unless it's on the list. (Don't sign for anything "promised later" – it may never turn up!)

■ make sure that equipment provided (like the fridge, cooker and heaters) actually works.

■ find out (and if possible, get in writing) who's responsible for repairs like drains or TV sets. These will usually be the owner's responsibility – but don't assume it.

■ check which (if any) facilities are shared with others and what costs may be involved.

■ ask whether you can decorate the place. If it's OK you'll usually have to pay for the materials yourself but sometimes the owner may chip in.

■ find out who's responsible for the upkeep of any gardens and don't let yourself in for cutting any grass unless the owner provides a lawnmower!

This is also your chance to check whether what you're getting is what you want and if it's worth the money. Think whether the heating looks adequate, if there's enough storage space or plug sockets. (Beware sockets for round-pin plugs – this means the place hasn't been rewired for years and is often a sign of neglect elsewhere.)

The agreement
It is in your interest to get as much as possible down in writing – but if you can, avoid signing the agreement unless you're sure what it means. Try and get anything that seems unclear or doubtful explained by an advice centre. If you don't have a written agreement, remember to ask the landlord or landlady:

■ the amount of notice you have to give when you want to quit and the amount the owner must give if he or she wants to get you out.

■ whether the agreement is for a fixed period (six months or a year for instance) or indefinite. You may well have fewer tenant's rights if the agreement is for six months.

■ what notice she or he will give before coming round. (Owners are allowed reasonable access to check you're not wrecking their property but shouldn't poke around your rooms or flat without your permission.)

■ if there are any rules (about keeping animals or having other people to stay for example).

■ whether you are a tenant or licensee (this affects your rights) and if you are a tenant or sub-tenant (is the person you're renting from the owner of the property or not?).

■ find out if the person you rent from lives in the property. If so it means fewer rights, if not then make sure you get an address where you can get in contact – many landlords or landladies try to vanish when you start asking about repairs.

■ check if the agreement includes meals. Unless you *want* to pay for full or half board, beware – even if the person you rent from says it's simply a formality. Just an unwanted box of cornflakes left on your doorstep once a week could affect your rights.

Once you're in

When you move into the first place of your own there are usually things you find you need but never thought of and which your new home hasn't got. If you can scrounge them from friends or family beforehand you'll save money and get comfortable sooner. Think about:

- a kettle, pots and pans
- an iron
- bed linen
- tea towels
- mugs, plates, cutlery
- adaptors for plug sockets.
- plenty of coathangers

Profile

"I've been living on my own now for nearly three years and the most useful things I've ever bought have been a couple of sharp knives for cooking and a tool kit for basic repairs – you know, just a screwdriver, a pair of pliers and a hammer. You never know when they'll be useful."

(Dave, 19, Shopworker)

If you need to furnish a place on the cheap, there's more than the sales and secondhand shops. Many towns also have auction rooms which do sales of ordinary furniture as opposed to antiques on a regular basis.

Fuel bills

If you have to feed a coin meter which your landlord or landlady empties then check you're not being overcharged. There are strict controls on the rates they can make you pay. Ask the electricity and gas boards for leaflets explaining this and if you believe you're paying too much see the Citizens' Advice Bureau about getting your money back through the courts.

When you move into a place tell the gas and electricity boards immediately. If you don't you could end up being charged for the previous occupant.

Keeping your fuel bills low is to some extent a matter of common sense like not having your heating on full and the windows wide open. Even so, some places are very difficult to heat – especially if the person who owns the property isn't bothered. Some of the things you can do include:

- check the roof is insulated. If it's not, remind the owner that grants are available towards materials and offer to do the work – it's not too difficult.

- make sure your water tank is insulated. If not get an eiderdown or old blankets from a jumble sale to wrap around it and tie on with string.
- keep room doors shut and draw curtains.
- if your pipes aren't lagged, wrap them in layers of newspaper.
- use clingfilm for instant cheap 'doubleglazing'.

Don't get too carried away though – rooms need ventilation, especially if there are gas fires.

Profile

"A couple of months after I moved into the flat, I got the sort of electricity bill that makes you think their computer's gone mad. But when I queried it they said it was right. Only then did I think that the water was probably on an immersion heater and that I'd never seen a switch for it. After I'd found the switch hidden in my airing cupboard I had to go and ask to pay this huge bill in instalments!

(Penny, 28, Administrator)

Insurance

This is one of life's less interesting subjects – until you wish you had thought about it. When you consider that your stereo, clothes and records alone may easily be worth several hundred pounds it begins to make sense. Shop around a few brokers to see who offers the best deals before you decide anything.

Your rights as a tenant

The law concerning your rights as a tenant is very complex. It depends on whether the property is owned privately, by the council or by an organisation like a housing association. It also depends on whether the owner lives on the property or not and on your particular agreement.

- If the landlord or landlady lives on the premises or provides board, you're likely to have a "restricted contract" which means you're not fully protected by the rent laws.
- If you're in lodgings or what your agreement calls "holiday accommodation" then you've hardly any protection.
- If you don't have a tenancy but a "licence to occupy" then you've only got limited protection.

■ If you're in a fixed–term letting called a "shorthold tenancy" your rights are different from other tenants.

The important thing if you have problems in rented accommodation is to get expert assistance quickly (seek advice from the nearest Citizens' Advice Bureau).

What follows are general guidelines only to common situations for private tenants. They are not intended to be a complete explanation of the law.

You're asked to quit

Unless you've taken a fixed–term tenancy which has come to the end of its time, you have to be given written notice to quit if you're a tenant (but not necessarily if you're a lodger or licencee). The written notice must contain certain information if it is valid and must give you at least four weeks warning. If you receive notice, get advice to see that it's correctly worded and to see if you're entitled to more time.

Even if the notice to quit is valid, the landlord or landlady can't simply enter your home to throw you or your possessions onto the street. The owner must get a court order before you can be evicted.

You think the rent is too high

The first thing to do is check with the Rent Office at your Town Hall to see if any previous tenants have had the rent registered within the past couple of years. If the place is registered and you're paying more, get advice about claiming money back from the owner. If your place isn't registered, check properties similar to yours in the area to see what their registered rent is. If you're paying less than the average don't do anything since the Rent Officer could put your rent up!

If you seem to be paying more than normal, you can ask the Rent Officer to fix a *Fair Rent* or a *Reasonable Rent* (which one depends on whether or not the landlord or landlady lives in the same property). Get details about what this involves plus advice from the Rent Office staff.

You can't get repairs done

Don't withhold your rent unless you've got advice first – otherwise you could break your tenancy agreement and give the owner a reason for evicting you.

The owner makes your life difficult
The legal word for this is "harassment" – and it's illegal even if the landlord or landlady wants you out. Cutting off your electricity, changing locks or any kind of threats may well be criminal offences – get help quickly.

Help for people with low incomes

All sorts of people are entitled to help with housing costs, whether they are in or out of work. The housing benefit scheme is run by local councils and includes rent rebates (for council tenants), rent allowances (for people paying rent to anyone else) and rate rebates (for people paying rates to the council – even if it's part of their rent).

If you have a low income or claim state benefits (such as the dole or family income supplement) you are probably eligible. There are different ways to get help, depending on your situation:

If you're on supplementary benefit
You don't need to make a separate claim for housing benefit, the social security office will pass your details directly to the local council if you're eligible (which most people are). You may be asked to fill in a form on your housing costs and arrangements to take to the local council which will then take responsibility for paying all your housing costs which are eligible. Council tenants won't be sent money – instead you'll just be charged less rent or no rent, depending on your entitlement. People renting privately will be sent a girocheque each month. This will be for two weeks in arrears and two weeks in advance. If you have to pay your rent every week, then you can get the allowance weekly – but only if you ask.

Virtually the only people on supplementary benefit who aren't entitled to housing benefit from the council are boarders in lodging houses, bed and breakfast accommodation or hostels. If this applies to you, you'll get extra supplementary benefit. Students claiming during vacations should contact their student union for details of special arrangements.

If you're living with your parents and are under 21, you won't get anything towards the rent. If you're 21 or more and live with your parents you get a very small contribution (£3.30 until November 1985).

If you're not on supplementary benefit
You will need to apply to the Housing Department of your local council if you're not claiming supplementary benefit. Whether you're sharing or in a hostel you may still be eligible. Even if you're working and receiving family income supplement you may be entitled to benefits. The rules about who qualifies are complex – so if you're on a low income for whatever reason, it's worth your while to claim.

If you're buying your home and lose your job
As well as claiming housing benefit for the interest element of your mortgage, you should also contact the organisation which lent you the money immediately. Building societies and bank will usually re-arrange your payments for a while if you've any prospect of finding another job. Only if there's no alternative will they ask you to sell up – but you've got to tell them if you can't meet the payments.

Help and advice

Places
Details of a few places to contact for information and help are given in the chapter, in addition try:
- *Your local council*. Ask for the Housing Department for details of council house allocation policy, housing associations which take people from the council waiting list and general information plus free leaflets about accommodation in your area and housing benefit. Ask for the Rent Officer if you think you're being overcharged.
- *Law Centres and Housing Advice Centres*. These are pretty much confined to big cities but will have useful leaflets and sympathetic advice on housing problems.
- *Citizens' Advice Bureaux*. Found in most towns and useful starting points for any housing questions. If you need legal aid, ask the CAB for details of schemes and solicitors.

The following organisations work on behalf of homeless people, produce several useful publications and have plenty of expertise:
- *Shelter (the National Campaign for the Homeless)*, 157 Waterloo Road, London SE1 8XF. Tel: 01 633 9377. Has regional centres in many other large towns.

- *CHAR (Campaign for Single Homeless People)*, 5–15 Cromer Street, London WC1H 8LS. Tel: 01 833 2071.
- *SHAC*, 189a Old Brompton Road, London SW5 0AR. Tel: 01 373 7841.

If you're in London with nowhere to stay, try the following places for details of where to find emergency shelter:

- *Alone in London Service*, Tel: 01 387 3010.
- *Piccadilly Advice Centre*, Subway 4, Piccadilly Station, London W1 Tel: 01 930 0066.

Publications

Housing Booklets (series of free pamphlets, published by the Department of the Environment). Cover most aspects of renting for both tenant and owner. Available from council offices and Citizens' Advice Bureau.

Housing and Supplementary Benefit (£2.80, from CHAR – address above). Particularly for single people. New editions published each November.

A Guide to Housing Benefit (£4.00, from SHAC – address above).

Squatters Handbook (42p. incl. post and package, from the Advisory Service for Squatters, 2 St. Pauls Road, London N1).

11. Time out

Getting around ■ buying transport ■ getting away ■ working abroad ■ working for free ■ sport ■ entertainment ■ help and advice

Getting around

No matter how much you like the place where you live, you won't want to be stuck there all the time. Travel can be a problem however – especially if you're on a low income or live in a rural area. Travelling under your own steam (either on foot or by cycling) is obviously cheap, healthy and won't cause any pollution. The problem is that it's also time consuming, only really an option for relatively short distances and is a real drag in bad weather. Despite the drawbacks, bikes are becoming increasingly popular – especially in cities.

Cycling
If you do cycle your main concern must be safety – you're very vulnerable to motor vehicles so:
■ keep your brakes in good nick (leather brake blocks are more expensive but work better in the wet)
■ get reflectors for your mudguard, your wheels and also a belt or sash reflector for yourself so that you're easily seen
■ use your lights in fog or at night otherwise you're asking for trouble (give dynamos a miss even though batteries are more expensive – most dynamo lights go out when you're stopped at a junction)
■ buy a bell and use it (pedestrians stepping off the kerb without looking can be a big hazard)
■ think about buying a helmet (most fatalities on bikes are the result of head injuries), it's extra expense and you may think you look a bit of a wally – but it could save your life
■ obey the highway code (it's often tempting to overtake slow moving cars on the inside, for example, but someone turning left is liable to smash into you).

Another major concern for cyclists is security. Never leave your bike unlocked unless you want to get it pinched. Buy the most expensive lock you can afford; solid steel ones are best – but fairly expensive at about £15, otherwise buy the thickest chain you can. Avoid the plastic-covered "wire strand" ones – they may deter a casual thief but otherwise they're easily cut. If you can, lock your bike through the frame to an immovable object (railings for example), lock the wheels too if they're the quick release type, also remove lights (especially batteries). Make a note of your bike's serial number (on the frame) because otherwise the police won't know it's yours if they recover it.

Try to keep down your cycling costs by doing your own repairs – most are pretty simple. You can either look for books in your local library or see if there are any evening classes. Some local groups of Friends of the Earth also run bike workshops to teach people maintenance.

Public transport

Usually much better services exist in cities than in rural areas where there may be no train stations for miles and already poor bus services may be under threat of closure.

If you're travelling the same route regularly, always ask about season tickets, returns, travelcards and other ways of cutting costs – they're well worth it.

If you're under twenty five (or older if you're a full time student) and travel by train, you'll almost certainly save money with a BR Young Persons' Railcard. Costing £12 a year, this allows you half-price second class fares on most journeys anywhere in Britain (exceptions include short journeys and trains from some main London stations during busy periods). Get details from most British Rail stations. Also look out for free ticket offers with washing powders!

Long distance coaches can be even cheaper than railcard fares on the train but aren't as comfortable and are more often delayed. Students may get discounts on many trips with the right identity cards – ask your student union about schemes or look out for leaflets at bus stations.

Taxis

A very expensive option. You may have to use taxis however if you miss the last bus and are worried about getting home safely. If you can, share taxis with as many other people as the driver will carry and try to travel before midnight after which time the meter simply eats up cash.

Hitching

When it goes well, hitch–hiking is speedy, free and interesting but when it goes badly you can wait hours for a ride which turns out to be with some kind of nutcase. Women hitchers face the greatest risks but men aren't always safe either. Whatever your sex, you're best off hitching with someone else and avoiding lifts where you're outnumbered.

Getting lifts depends to some extent on luck – but also on being in the best position. For best results:

■ don't waste your time hitching in cities
■ don't hitch in front of major junctions or roundabouts – go to the turnoff
■ don't hitch on bends
■ on straight stretches of road, give drivers time to slow down and pull up (so don't wait at lay-bys, walk back about fifty metres)
■ don't hitch on motorway slip roads (in practice this may be hard to avoid but the police will kick you off if they see you)
■ do talk to other hitchers – you'll often pick up good tips for particular routes and it helps pass the time.

Some people like to use a destination card (especially for long trips), others prefer pot luck. One way to cut down on the risks of bad experiences when hitching is not to say where you're going but ask where the driver's going – then if you don't like the look of him or her it's easier to refuse by saying it's not your direction.

Your car or motorbike

This can be expensive but your own motor transport means the freedom to travel when and where you want. Before you go out on the road, you should make sure that you're within the law.

Whether or not it's yours, the vehicle you use must have a current tax disc and a Ministry of Transport (MOT) certificate if it's over three years old. In addition, you must have:

A licence: This must be valid for the type of vehicle you want to drive. You have to be at least sixteen to ride a moped (engine under

50 cc.) and seventeen to ride a motorcycle or drive a car. For heavy goods vehicles you must be over twenty one. Get an application form from most Post Offices. If you've not passed a driving test for that type of vehicle there are other restrictions:

- you must display L plates
- you can't ride bikes with engines over 125 cc.
- you must have someone who holds a full driving licence with you in cars
- you mustn't have someone with you on a bike unless he or she has passed their bike test. You can ride a moped with a car licence however.

Current insurance: You must have at least "third party insurance" before you take a vehicle onto a public road. This will cover you if you cause any injury or damage to other people. In addition you may choose to pay more and be covered if your car or bike is stolen or damaged. What you'll have to pay for insurance depends on things like:

- where you live
- your age
- the make and model of the vehicle.

If you're riding a motorbike or moped, you'll also need a helmet (unless you're a Sikh). Buy the best you can afford – it could save your life. Watch out for cracks in secondhand helmets and don't put paint or stickers on your helmet since the chemicals could weaken the plastic so that it doesn't give you proper protection. You'll also need protective clothing. If you can afford leathers, buy them – don't think about style, it's protection you want and leather is far better than trainers, jeans and a jacket if you come off a bike at speed.

Buying transport

Unless you're rich or know someone very generous, the first transport you buy is likely to be secondhand. When money's tight it's even more important to get a good deal but it's easy to make mistakes. Probably the best advice is to talk to friends who've bought before and know some of the pitfalls – and if you can, get them to go along with you when you're thinking of buying.

Cycles

Private sales through adverts in shop windows or local papers should be the best bargains. You should also check with your local police to see if they auction off unclaimed bikes they take in. When you buy, it's best to check:

■ that the frame's not been in a crash (wrinkled paintwork at the top of the front forks is usually a sign that they've been straightened)

■ the wheels aren't buckled and that they spin freely

■ that the brakes work

■ that the cranks are straight and don't wobble from side to side.

Always get a receipt if you buy and since it's difficult to prove the ownership of bikes, don't buy if anything about the deal gives you cause to suspect the bike's been stolen.

Motorcycles and mopeds

Local papers and the motorcycle press will have good deals. Avoid old British or East European models unless you're a real enthusiast – spares are often very difficult to get and the engines are often unreliable at the best of times. Always check for bent footrests as these can be a sign that the bike's been in an accident. Oil leaks and a loose chain are other bad signs. Always take a test ride before buying.

Cars

Whether you buy from a dealer or privately, it's best to be very cautious – sometimes what looks like a good deal can turn out to be nothing but trouble.

Don't be tempted by big cars at very cheap prices. It might be stylish to own a Jag but the insurance costs will be huge and it'll drink up petrol. Always check likely insurance costs of different models with your insurance company. Beware also of less popular makes as getting spares can be very time consuming – go for the more popular cars like Minis, Escorts and Metros which are easy to service yourself. Avoid automatics too – if the transmission goes wrong you're unlikely to be able to repair it yourself and it can be very expensive.

What you should be looking for is a car which has had one or two careful owners – not an ex-company car. Although garage and dealer prices may be higher, you should be able to get a guarantee from reputable places which can be worth it. Car auctions can be cheap but unless you're with someone who knows the ropes you could end up by buying an expensive scrapheap. Think twice about buying from friends – if something goes wrong then there can be all sorts of bad feeling.

When you go out looking at cars check:

- on the roof for any sign of a driving school sign having been removed (remember what *you* used to do to the gearbox when you learned to drive!)
- the door panels for signs of painted–over company adverts
- the mats, carpets and pedals for wear (sales reps will have been in and out of their cars a lot)
- for signs of re–sprays and bodywork repairs (watch out for fibreglass repairs)
- for rust – particularly round the doors and underneath, it can't be cured, may spread and is expensive to treat
- the condition of the tyres and amount of tread
- under the bonnet.

But remember, many faults won't show up on any check you can do.

Always ask:

- why the person wants to sell the car (you may not get the truth though)
- for details of the car's service record (to check it's been looked after)
- to see the MOT certificate if it's older than three years. Think very hard about the risks of buying a car without an MOT.

Always take the car out for a test run if it looks worth buying and be sure to drive it in all gears (including reverse).

If you or someone you know is in a motoring organisation, you may be able to arrange for a mechanic to check over a car you want to buy (for a fee). Don't let the person selling rush you into making a deal and don't buy if he or she doesn't have the registration document (it may not be that person's car at all).

If you do go ahead and buy, pay by cheque if you can – that way you may be able to stop the cheque if the car falls apart immediately after you've driven off.

It's easy to get a bad deal when buying secondhand – so while you're still planning, use the motoring section in your library, car magazines and publications like *Which* (see Chapter 5, *Managing*

money) to pick up more tips. For prices, look at magazines like
Parker's Car Price Guide, Motorists' Guide and *Used Car Prices*.

Profile

"I bought an old Daf from my sister's boyfriend – it looked like a real
bargain at £450, six year old. It had quite a long MOT too.
Everything was fine for about three months and then just about
anything which can go wrong with a car did – within the space of
about six weeks. It was one repair bill after another. I'd spent more
on repairs than I'd spent on the car in the first place before I gave up.
I traded it in part-exchange with a dealer and bought a Cortina but
really pity the person who's got it now."

Stevie (20, Baker)

Getting away

Although you don't need to leave the UK to get away for a while,
this section is about cheap travel abroad.

Passports and visas

For virtually all travel outside Britain you'll need a passport. There
are three sorts:

- a standard passport (valid for ten years and costing £15)
- a British Visitor's passport (only accepted in some countries –
  but these do include the EEC, valid for one year only and costing
  £7.50).
- a British Excursion passport (valid for one month, for visits to
  France, costing £2).

Get application forms from main Post Offices and send them off to
the address given well in advance of when you want to travel (at
least a month – longer in summer). You'll also need two photos (use
the booths which say "passport approved" and the signature of
someone in the local community who's known you for a couple of
years. You're meant to use people like doctors, lawyers and teachers
for this but many doctors will ask you to pay for their autograph. If
you don't have friends in high status jobs don't worry – there are
stories of some people who've got away with asking their milkman!
(And why not?)

Visas won't be needed for holiday visits to Western Europe but if
you're going further afield or travelling as part of your work, you'll

probably have to have them. Find out before you go from your travel agent or the Embassy of the country you want to visit (requirements can change very quickly so make sure your information is up to date). You can find details of Embassies in reference books like the *Statesman's Yearbook* and *Whitaker's Almanac* in most libraries.

Hitching abroad
If you can speak the language, great – but even if you can't it's possible and can be a really interesting way of seeing a country (though the risks are still there and may increase the further you get from the UK). Think twice and think again about hitching in the USA if you're lucky enough to get that far – it's probably not a good idea. If you make it down to the Mediterranean you could get lucky hitching on private boats in return for work. Look at the books in *Help and advice* for more tips about hitching abroad and watch out for laws about hitching on or even near motorways.

Package tours
Lots of people look down on package tourists and prefer to travel independently but package holidays can turn out to be the best value for money of all – particularly if you go right at the start or end of the season. Some people even claim it's worth taking the package travel and then going off on your own rather than sitting in a crummy resort hotel. There's nothing wrong with package tours if that's what you want, but since most of the travel industry can provide free information, they're not covered in any detail here.

Coaches
Usually fairly cheap compared to trains or planes but can be slow and uncomfortable. Wide variety from beat-up old buses to luxury air-conditioned coaches with loos, refreshments and videos (though the choice of videos is always lousy). Shop around for the best bargains – go to a number of travel agents and look out for adverts in national papers (*The Guardian, The Times*) and magazines like *Time Out, City Limits, New Statesman* or *Private Eye*.

Trains
If you're under 26 you can get cheap rail travel in Europe through Transalpino (up to 50% off). If your travel agent doesn't have

details, ring Transalpino on 01 828 6440/6421 for information.
There's also the Inter–Rail card which you can buy at mainline
stations. You have to be under 26 so take proof of your age. For £119
you get half price travel in the country you buy the card plus
unlimited free travel on most European railways (including several
East European countries) for one month.

Air travel

Regulations and prices are very, very complicated but with a bit of
work and a flexible schedule you need never pay the standard fare.
Check first for advance booking prices, then ask about youth and
student fares. You can sometimes pick up "standby" tickets cheaply
if you don't mind waiting. In London, look out for small adverts in
the press from "bucket shops" (small specialists in off-loading
tickets which the airlines can't sell) which just about stay inside the
regulations.

   If you're not worried about when you fly and can travel light, try
contacting courier firms near the major airports – you'll sometimes
be able to pick up a free or subsidised flight for delivering
documents or small parcels. You have to be ready to go when
required though.

Insurance and money

If you fall ill when abroad you could have major problems if you're
not insured. In the EEC and a few other countries things aren't too
bad but otherwise you're in trouble. It's well worth taking out some
insurance when you go abroad so that your trip's not ruined
entirely. Ask your travel agent for details or ask an insurance broker
(look in yellow pages under "I") about different types. It's also
worth asking the DHSS for leaflet SA.30 *Medical costs abroad: what
you need to know before you go* and SA.35 which has details of what
vaccinations you may need and special precautions to take. If you're
going to the EEC, fill in the form attached to SA.30 about four
weeks before you leave to get a certificate (E111) which will make
things simpler if you fall ill.

   Carrying large amounts of cash when you're abroad isn't the
most sensible thing to do. If it's lost or stolen then you've had it. The
way to get round this is carry your money in travellers' cheques
which can be converted into cash at banks (and many hotels). You
don't have to have a bank account to buy travellers' cheques but

there will be a small commission charge. If you lose your travellers' cheques and report it to an office of the company which sold them to you (or their foreign agent) you'll be able to get a refund fairly quickly.

Travellers' cheques are issued by banks and companies like Thomas Cook and American Express and are available in pounds, dollars or other currencies. Get advice when you buy as to which sorts are most acceptable in the country you're visiting.

Your credit card may also be valid abroad and can be helpful in emergencies and always carry enough cash on you for immediate needs (banks abroad may have different opening times).

Accommodation

If you've not booked ahead you've got to be prepared to spend time looking for somewhere to stay – and this can be hard in major tourist centres although for some people it's part of the challenge of independent travel. In some countries they won't let you over the border unless you've got somewhere to stay or accommodation vouchers – check before you leave! Youth Hostels are usually good value basic accommodation (in Britain as well as abroad) but in capital cities they fill up very quickly. Cheap hotels are often not much more expensive (especially if you can persuade the owner to let four of you share a room!).

Joining the Youth Hostels Association isn't very expensive. Write to the YHA, Trevelyan House, St. Steven's Hill, St. Albans, Herts. AL1 2DY. Tel: (0727) 55215.

Working abroad

This is seldom easy during times of high unemployment when most countries are trying to provide jobs for their own citizens but it's not impossible. Some countries simply won't let you in to work unless you've got specialist skills, the right visa and work permit but things are a bit easier within the EEC (though there may still be formalities). Unless you've got a skill in high demand your chances of full-time legitimate work are slim but you may be able to pick up low paid casual work (often cash-in-hand) around tourist resorts and in the hotel and catering trade.

If you only want to work for a short period (such as a summer vacation) things are a little easier and you may be able to find jobs grape-picking in France or Italy, work with children in US summer camps or camp-site attendant work in Spain.

For more information, look at the books mentioned in *Help and advice*.

Other ways of working abroad are as an au pair or as a volunteer. See *Help and advice* for books with this information.

In the long term, you may think about emigrating to a new country – contact its embassy in this country for details.

Working for free

If you've got time on your hands, one way to use it is to help others. This may mean:

- disabled people
- victims of war, famine or political oppression
- elderly people
- self-help to improve things for people like you or in your neighbourhood
- children
- conserving the environment for everyone's benefit.

You'll be lucky to get much money for doing this (though you may be able to get expenses in many cases) but it's still a valuable way of increasing your experiences, expanding your social life and contacts and the work itself can be really satisfying as you are doing something you think is worthwhile. You may even find that this sort of work is more interesting than any paid job you may have.

You should be able to find something which suits your interests and abilities, whether it's: out of doors or in an office; working with other people or with animals; writing, talking, travelling, using artistic skill or using muscle power; in your neighbourhood or further away (maybe even abroad); just for a couple of hours a week or full-time for a year.

For part-time opportunities locally, contact your county or borough's Council for Voluntary Service (in some areas it's called a Community Council or Guild for Voluntary Organisations). If you can't find anything in the phone book under your borough, county or region name, ask the Citizens' Advice Bureau or at your library. Many councils for voluntary service will have a Volunteer's Bureau or someone who handles enquiries – but even if they don't they should be able to send you a list of the various organisations in membership so that you can approach likely ones yourself. If there doesn't seem to be a local branch of the sort of organisation you want to help, look at *Voluntary Organisations: an NCVO Directory*, published by the National Council for Voluntary Organisations which should be in most libraries. This has details of all the major organisations in this area.

There are likely to be lots of other local projects – particularly self-help ones. Ask neighbours, local youth workers, community centre staff, community relations councils, women's groups and libraries if they know of groups or individuals who could use some help.

Longer term volunteering

If you can give up between four and twelve months of your time and commit them to a project, there's an organisation called Community Service Volunteers which can fix you up with somewhere to work, pay your board and lodging and give you travel expenses plus a small weekly allowance. They never turn anyone down. The sort of work you could do includes arts projects, providing care for someone with a physical disability, working in children's homes or youth clubs, work with alcoholics or ex-prisoners. Sometimes the work isn't easy but almost everyone who becomes a volunteer will say they found the time well spent.

Look in the phone book to see if there's a local office near you or write to CSV, 237 Pentonville Road, London N1 9NJ. Tel: 01 278 6601.

Other organisations organise longer term opportunities too, including ones overseas. Increasingly you need particular skills or qualifications (or be able to pay) to go on programmes in the Third World which are for a year or more but there are also projects and work camps lasting just a few months in Europe. These will usually provide board and lodging but may not be able to pay your travel costs or give you an allowance. Look at the book *Working Abroad* (details in *Help and advice*).

Sport and entertainment

There are two ways to approach these – as a spectator or as a participant. If you simply watch sports or go to concerts or films there's not really too much to say – except always try for discounts if you're a student or claimant. Remember though, you don't have to sit on the sidelines, it's usually possible to get involved yourself.

Sport

Sport isn't something you have to stop once you leave school. It's a way of staying fit throughout your life. You could either keep up or rediscover something you enjoyed earlier in your life or you could try something new. You may want to work on an individual activity like swimming or weight training or have a go at something more competitive like volleyball, badminton or tennis. For some sports, it's probably a bit late to launch a career as an international athlete but there are others where you *can* achieve success without having done it since you were a child.

There are some competitive sports where the main thing is to prove your capability to yourself – marathon running is probably the best example.

While some sports require lots of equipment and facilities which may be a bit expensive there are plenty which can be done on the cheap. Local councils have pools, pitches and centres all over the country and the clubs and individuals using them are often very keen to welcome new people to join them. If you want more instruction, try to join a group that's organised as an evening class because then it'll often be free or cheap if you're out of work.

Local libraries usually have details of sports clubs and facilities. For more general information, contact: the Sports Council, 16 Upper Woburn Place, London WC1. Tel: 01 388 1277. The Sports Council for Wales, Sophia Gardens, Cardiff CF1 9SW. Tel: (0222) 397571. The Sports Council for Northern Ireland, 49 Malone Road, Belfast BT9 6RZ. Tel: (0232) 663154. The Scottish Sports Council, 1 St. Colne Street, Edinburgh EH13 6AA. Tel: 031 225 8411.

Entertainment

While there are some forms of entertainment, like dances, where you participate there's lots more where you may think there's not a lot you can do except watch – but you'd be wrong.

If you *can* sing, tell jokes, play music or act then try working up a routine and doing performances. If you've never tried any of those activities you could give them a go. Just about every town has an amateur dramatic group, music society or local bands (and if they haven't or you don't like what's available, try advertising in your local paper to see if others feel the same way and can help you set up an alternative).

Even if your talents don't lie in those areas you can still try your hand at promoting events on your own or with others (either for fun or as a way of making a bit of money).

Help and advice

Hitchhiking
For tips and directions, look at:
- *Hitchhikers Manual: Britain* and *Europe: a Manual for Hitchhikers* both by Simon Calder, published by Vacation Work Publications, 9 Park End Street, Oxford OX1 1HJ. Tel: (0865) 241978, £4.25 including post and packing.
- the *Hitchhiker's Guide to Europe* by Ken Welsh, published by Pan Books from any bookshop, £2.95. Full of hints and advice.

Working abroad
One of the most useful books on the subject is *Working Abroad* by Godfrey Golzen, published by Kogan Page Ltd., £5.95 (paperback).

For more short-term opportunities look at Vacation Work Publications (address above) like:
- *Directory of Jobs and Careers Abroad*
- *Work your way around the world.*

If you're a student and want to try work in an American Summer Camp, try BUNAC, 30 Store Street, London WC1E 7BS. Tel: 01 637 7686.

Voluntary work
For voluntary work overseas, look at:
- *International Directory of Voluntary Work*
- *Kibbutz Volunteer*

published by Vacation Work Publications (above)
- *Volunteer Work Abroad*
- *Working Holidays*

published by the *Central Bureau for Educational Visits and Exchanges*, Seymour Mews House, Seymour Mews, London W1H 9PE. Tel: 01 486 5101 (also offices in Belfast and Edinburgh).

Useful organisations include:

■ *British Volunteer Programme*, 22 Coleman Fields, London W1Y 2AA. Tel: 01 226 6616.

■ *Voluntary Service Overseas*, 9 Belgrave Square, London SW1X 8PW. Tel: 01 235 5191.

For opportunities in Britain, contact your local *Council for Voluntary Service, Community Service Volunteers* (address in section) or try the *Volunteer Centre*, 29 Lower King's Road, Berkhamsted, Herts. HP4 2AB. Tel: (04427) 73311. This organisation acts as a focus for voluntary activity and produces publications but does *not* recruit individual volunteers.

Index